"Mastering Time: Unlocking the Secrets of
Effective Time Management"
By:Amal Alaa

Table of Contents

Table of contents:

1. Introduction to Time Management

Time management is a crucial skill that plays a significant role in our personal and professional lives. It refers to the process of planning, organizing, and controlling how we allocate our time to different activities and tasks. Effective time management allows us to make the most of our limited time and achieve our goals efficiently.

The importance of time management cannot be overstated. In today's fast-paced world, where distractions are abundant and demands on our time are ever-increasing, being able to manage our time effectively is essential for success. Whether it is meeting deadlines at work, balancing work and personal life, or pursuing personal goals, time management helps us stay focused, productive, and in control.

One of the key benefits of time management is increased productivity. When we manage our time well, we are able to prioritize tasks, set realistic goals, and allocate appropriate time to each activity. This allows us to work more efficiently and accomplish more in less time. By avoiding procrastination and staying organized, we can minimize distractions and stay on track, leading to higher productivity and better outcomes.

Time management also helps reduce stress and improve work-life balance. When we have a clear plan and schedule, we can allocate time for work, leisure, and personal activities. This helps prevent burnout and allows us to maintain a healthy work-life balance. By managing our time effectively, we can ensure that we have time for ourselves, our loved ones, and activities that bring us joy and fulfillment.

Furthermore, time management enhances decision-making and problem-solving skills. When we have a good grasp of our priorities and deadlines, we can make informed decisions about how to allocate our time and resources. This enables us to make better choices and avoid overcommitting ourselves. Additionally, effective time management allows us to anticipate and address potential challenges and obstacles in a timely manner, leading to better problem-solving and decision-making.

In conclusion, time management is a fundamental skill that is essential for success in all aspects of life. By planning, organizing, and controlling our time effectively, we can increase productivity, reduce stress, improve work-life balance, and enhance decision-making skills. Developing and honing our time management skills is a lifelong process that requires self-discipline, focus, and commitment. However, the benefits of effective time management are well worth the effort, as it allows us to make the most of our time and achieve our goals with greater efficiency and satisfaction.

1. Understanding the Importance of Time Management

Time management is a crucial skill that plays a significant role in our personal and professional lives. It refers to the ability to allocate and utilize time effectively and efficiently to accomplish tasks, meet deadlines, and achieve goals. Understanding the importance of time management can have numerous benefits and can positively impact various aspects of our lives. Here are a few reasons why time management is essential:

Increased productivity: Effective time management allows individuals to prioritize tasks and focus on important activities. By allocating time wisely, individuals can accomplish more in less time, leading to increased productivity and efficiency.

Reduced stress: Poor time management often leads to stress and anxietyWhen individuals fail to manage their time effectively, they may feel overwhelmed by the number of tasks and deadlinesBy practicing good time management, individuals can reduce stress levels and maintain a better work-life balance.

Improved decision-making: Time management enables individuals to allocate sufficient time for decision-makingWhen individuals have enough time to evaluate options and make informed decisions, they are more likely to make better choices and achieve desired outcomes.

Enhanced quality of work: When individuals manage their time effectively, they can allocate sufficient time to complete tasks accurately and with attention to detailThis leads to improved quality of work and reduces the chances of errors or mistakes.

Increased opportunities: Effective time management allows individuals to make the most of their time and seize opportunities as they ariseBy being proactive and organized, individuals can create space for new opportunities and make progress towards their goals.

Better work-life balance: Time management helps individuals strike a balance between work and personal lifeBy allocating time for both professional and personal activities, individuals can maintain a healthy and fulfilling lifestyle.

Improved self-discipline: Time management requires self-discipline and the ability to prioritize tasksBy practicing time management, individuals can develop self-discipline, which can be beneficial in various aspects of life.

In conclusion, understanding the importance of time management is crucial for personal and professional success. By effectively managing time, individuals can increase productivity, reduce stress, make better decisions, improve the quality of work, seize opportunities, maintain a work-life balance, and develop self-discipline. It is a skill that can be learned and honed over time, and its benefits are well worth the effort.

1. Assessing Your Current Time Management Skills

Assessing your current time management skills can be a helpful exercise to identify areas for improvement and develop strategies to become more efficient and productive. Here are a few steps you can follow to assess your time management skills:

Evaluate your current time management practices: Take some time to reflect on how you currently manage your time. Consider the strategies and techniques you use, such as creating to-do lists, setting priorities, and using time-blocking techniques. Assess how effective these practices are in helping you stay organized and meet deadlines.

Identify your strengths and weaknesses: Think about the areas where you excel in managing your time and the areas where you struggleFor example, you may be good at setting goals and prioritizing tasks but struggle with avoiding distractions or estimating the time required for each taskIdentifying your strengths and weaknesses will help you focus on areas that need improvement.

Track your time: Keep a record of how you spend your time for a few days or a weekThis can be done using a time-tracking app or simply by writing down your activities and the time spent on eachThis will give you a clear picture of how you allocate your time and identify any time-wasting activities or patterns.

Analyze your time usage: Once you have tracked your time, analyze the data to identify patterns and areas where you can make improvementsLook for tasks that take up a significant amount of time but don't contribute much to your goalsAlso, identify any time gaps or periods of low productivity that can be utilized more effectively.

Set goals and prioritize: Based on your analysis, set specific goals for improving your time management skillsBreak these goals down into smaller, actionable stepsPrioritize these steps based on their impact and feasibilityThis will help you focus on the most important areas and make progress towards your goals.

Implement new strategies: Start implementing the strategies and techniques you have identified to improve your time management skillsThis may include setting clear deadlines, using productivity tools, delegating tasks, or practicing better time estimationExperiment with different approaches and adjust as needed.

Monitor and adjust: Regularly monitor your progress and make adjustments as neededAssess the effectiveness of the new strategies you have implemented and make changes if necessaryTime management is an ongoing process, so be open to trying new techniques and refining your approach.

Remember, improving time management skills takes time and practice. Be patient with yourself and celebrate small victories along the way.

1. Setting SMART Goals for Effective Time Management

Setting SMART goals is a great way to improve time management skills. SMART is an acronym that stands for Specific, Measurable, Achievable, Relevant, and Time-bound. By following these guidelines, you can create goals that are clear, trackable, and realistic. Here's how you can set SMART goals for effective time management:

Specific: Clearly define what you want to achieve. Be specific about the task or outcome you want to accomplish. For example, instead of saying "I want to be more productive," specify "I want to complete all my assigned tasks by the end of the day."

Measurable: Set goals that can be measuredDefine how you will track your progress and determine whether you have achieved your goalFor example, if your goal is to improve time management, you can measure it by tracking the number of tasks completed within a specific time frame.

Achievable: Ensure that your goals are realistic and attainableConsider your current workload, resources, and capabilitiesSetting goals that are too ambitious may lead to frustration and burnoutBreak down larger goals into smaller, manageable tasks to make them more achievable.

Relevant: Set goals that are relevant to your overall objectives and prioritiesAlign your goals with your long-term plans and valuesAsk yourself if the goal is meaningful and contributes to your personal or professional growth.

Time-bound: Set a deadline for your goalsHaving a specific timeframe creates a sense of urgency and helps you stay focusedIt also allows you to prioritize tasks and allocate your time effectivelyFor example, set a deadline to complete a specific task by the end of the week.

By setting SMART goals, you can enhance your time management skills and work towards achieving your objectives in a more organized and efficient manner. Remember to regularly review and adjust your goals as needed to stay on track.

5-Prioritizing Tasks and Activities

Prioritizing tasks and activities is an essential skill for effective time management and productivity. Here are some strategies to help you prioritize your tasks:

Make a to-do list: Start by listing all the tasks and activities you need to complete. This will give you a clear overview of what needs to be done.

Determine urgency and importance: Assess the urgency and importance of each taskUrgent tasks are those that have a deadline or require immediate attentionImportant tasks are those that align with your goals and have a significant impact on your work or personal life.

Use the Eisenhower Matrix: The Eisenhower Matrix is a popular tool for prioritizationIt categorizes tasks into four quadrants based on their urgency and importance:

- Quadrant 1: Urgent and important tasks. These tasks should be your top priority and need to be addressed immediately.

- Quadrant 2: Important but not urgent tasks. These tasks should be planned and scheduled to prevent them from becoming urgent in the future.

- Quadrant 3: Urgent but not important tasks. These tasks can be delegated or minimized to free up time for more important activities.

- Quadrant 4: Not urgent and not important tasks. These tasks should be eliminated or postponed as they do not contribute to your goals.

4. Consider deadlines and dependencies: Take into account any deadlines or dependencies when prioritizing tasks. Tasks with approaching deadlines or tasks that are dependent on others should be given higher priority.

5. Assess your energy and focus levels: Consider your energy and focus levels when prioritizing tasks. Prioritize tasks that require high levels of concentration or creativity when you are most alert and focused.

6. Break down complex tasks: If you have complex tasks, break them down into smaller, manageable sub-tasks. This will make it easier to prioritize and complete them.

7. Reevaluate and adjust priorities: Regularly review and adjust your priorities as new tasks or changes occur. Flexibility is key to effective prioritization.

Remember, prioritization is a personal process, and what works for one person may not work for another. Experiment with different strategies and find the approach that works best for you.

1. Creating a Daily and Weekly Schedule

Creating a Daily and Weekly Schedule

A well-structured daily and weekly schedule is essential for managing time effectively and achieving personal and professional goals. By creating a schedule, individuals can prioritize tasks, allocate time for important activities, and maintain a sense of balance in their lives. In this essay, we will explore the benefits of having a daily and weekly schedule and provide practical tips for creating an effective one.

One of the primary advantages of having a daily and weekly schedule is that it helps individuals stay organized and focused. When we have a clear plan for each day and week, we can avoid wasting time on unimportant tasks and ensure that we allocate sufficient time for important activities. By prioritizing tasks and setting specific time slots for each activity, we can increase productivity and accomplish more in less time.

Moreover, a well-structured schedule allows individuals to maintain a healthy work-life balance. By allocating time for work, personal activities, and leisure, we can avoid burnout and ensure that we have time for self-care and relaxation. A balanced schedule helps us avoid overworking and allows us to enjoy our personal lives without neglecting our professional responsibilities.

To create an effective daily and weekly schedule, it is important to follow a few key principles. Firstly, it is essential to identify and prioritize tasks based on their importance and urgency. By categorizing tasks into different levels of priority, we can ensure that we focus on the most critical activities first. This helps prevent procrastination and ensures that important tasks are completed on time.

Secondly, it is important to allocate sufficient time for each task. By estimating the time required for each activity, we can create a realistic schedule that allows for adequate completion of tasks. It is crucial to avoid overloading the schedule and allow for flexibility to accommodate unexpected events or delays.

Additionally, it is beneficial to create a routine by scheduling similar activities at the same time each day or week. This helps establish a sense of structure and makes it easier to develop good habits. For example, setting a specific time for exercise each day can help individuals maintain a consistent fitness routine.

Furthermore, it is important to review and adjust the schedule regularly. As priorities and commitments change, it is necessary to adapt the schedule accordingly. By regularly evaluating the effectiveness of the schedule and making necessary adjustments, individuals can ensure that their schedule remains relevant and aligned with their goals.

In conclusion, creating a daily and weekly schedule is crucial for effective time management and achieving personal and professional goals. A well-structured schedule helps individuals stay organized, prioritize tasks, and maintain a healthy work-life balance. By following key principles such as prioritizing tasks, allocating sufficient time, creating routines, and regularly reviewing the schedule, individuals can create an effective schedule that maximizes productivity and enhances overall well-being.

1. Overcoming Procrastination

Procrastination is a common challenge that many people face. It refers to the act of delaying or postponing tasks or actions that need to be done. Overcoming procrastination requires self-awareness, discipline, and effective strategies. Here are some tips to help you overcome procrastination:

Set Clear Goals: Clearly define what you want to achieve and set specific, measurable, achievable, relevant, and time-bound (SMART) goals. Having a clear sense of direction will motivate you to take action.

Break Tasks into Smaller Steps: Large tasks can be overwhelming and lead to procrastinationBreak them down into smaller, manageable stepsThis will make the tasks more approachable and less intimidating.

Prioritize Tasks: Identify the most important tasks and prioritize them based on their urgency and importanceFocus on completing high-priority tasks first to avoid procrastination.

Create a Schedule: Develop a schedule or to-do list that outlines your tasks and deadlinesThis will help you stay organized and accountableSet aside dedicated time for each task and stick to the schedule.

Eliminate Distractions: Minimize distractions that can hinder your productivityTurn off notifications on your phone, close unnecessary tabs on your computer, and create a quiet and clutter-free workspace.

Use Time Management Techniques: Explore different time management techniques, such as the Pomodoro Technique or time blockingThese techniques can help you manage your time effectively and stay focused.

Find Your Motivation: Identify what motivates you and use it as a driving force to overcome procrastinationWhether it's a reward system, visualizing the end result, or seeking support from others, find what works best for you.

Overcome Perfectionism: Perfectionism can often lead to procrastinationAccept that not everything needs to be perfect and focus on progress rather than perfectionDone is better than perfect.

Seek Accountability: Share your goals and progress with someone you trust, such as a friend, family member, or mentorHaving someone hold you accountable can help you stay motivated and committed to completing your tasks.

Practice Self-Care: Take care of your physical and mental well-beingGet enough sleep, eat a balanced diet, exercise regularly, and manage stressWhen you feel good, you are more likely to stay focused and productive.

Remember, overcoming procrastination is a journey that requires consistent effort and self-reflection. Be patient with yourself and celebrate your progress along the way.

8-Dealing with Time Wasters

Dealing with time wasters can be challenging, but there are several strategies you can use to effectively manage your time and minimize their impact. Here are some tips to help you deal with time wasters:

Identify the time wasters: The first step is to identify the activities or behaviors that are wasting your time. This could include excessive social media use, unnecessary meetings, or interruptions from colleagues.

Set clear goals and priorities: By setting clear goals and priorities, you can focus your time and energy on the most important tasksThis will help you avoid getting sidetracked by time-wasting activities.

Create a schedule: Develop a schedule or to-do list that outlines your daily tasks and activitiesThis will help you stay organized and ensure that you allocate time for important tasks.

Learn to say no: It's important to learn to say no to requests or tasks that are not aligned with your goals or prioritiesThis will help you avoid taking on unnecessary work that can waste your time.

Minimize distractions: Identify and minimize distractions in your work environmentThis could include turning off notifications on your phone or computer, closing unnecessary tabs or apps, and creating a quiet and focused workspace.

Delegate tasks: If possible, delegate tasks to others who are capable of completing themThis will free up your time to focus on more important or high-priority tasks.

Use technology to your advantage: There are many productivity tools and apps available that can help you manage your time more effectivelyExplore options such as task management apps, time tracking tools, and calendar apps to find what works best for you.

Take breaks: It's important to take regular breaks to rest and rechargeThis will help you maintain focus and productivity throughout the day.

Communicate expectations: Clearly communicate your expectations to colleagues and team membersLet them know your availability and preferred methods of communication to minimize interruptions and time-wasting interactions.

Continuous improvement: Regularly evaluate your time management strategies and make adjustments as neededReflect on what is working well and what can be improved to optimize your productivity.

By implementing these strategies, you can effectively deal with time wasters and make the most of your time. Remember, time is a valuable resource, so it's important to use it wisely.

9- Managing Distractions and Interruptions

To manage distractions and interruptions effectively, here are some strategies you can follow:

Create a Distraction-Free Environment:

- Find a quiet and comfortable place to work where you can minimize external distractions.

- Turn off notifications on your phone or computer to avoid being interrupted by incoming messages or alerts.

- Use noise-cancelling headphones or play background music to block out noise if needed.

2. Prioritize and Plan Your Tasks:

- Make a to-do list or use a task management tool to prioritize your tasks and allocate specific time slots for each task.

- Break down larger tasks into smaller, more manageable chunks to avoid feeling overwhelmed.

- Identify your most important tasks and focus on completing them first before moving on to less critical ones.

3. Set Clear Boundaries:

- Communicate your availability and boundaries to colleagues, family members, or roommates to minimize interruptions during designated work hours.

- Use a "Do Not Disturb" sign or a similar visual cue to indicate when you need uninterrupted time.

4. Practice Time Blocking:

- Allocate specific blocks of time for focused work without any distractions or interruptions.

- Use a timer or productivity app to track your time and stay on track.

5. Use Productivity Tools:

- Utilize productivity tools and apps that can help you stay focused and manage distractions, such as task managers, Pomodoro timers, or website blockers.

- Consider using browser extensions that block access to distracting websites or limit your time spent on them.

6. Take Regular Breaks:

- Schedule short breaks throughout your workday to give yourself time to recharge and prevent burnout.

- Use these breaks to stretch, walk around, or engage in activities that help you relax and clear your mind.

7. Practice Mindfulness:

- Develop mindfulness techniques, such as deep breathing exercises or meditation, to help you stay present and focused on your tasks.

- When distractions arise, acknowledge them without judgment and gently redirect your attention back to your work.

Remember, managing distractions and interruptions requires discipline and consistency. It may take time to develop these habits, but with practice, you can improve your ability to stay focused and productive.

10-Effective Planning and Organization Techniques

Sure! Here are some effective planning and organization techniques:

Set Clear Goals: Start by setting clear and specific goals for what you want to achieve. This will help you stay focused and motivated.

Prioritize Tasks: Prioritize your tasks based on their importance and urgencyUse techniques like the Eisenhower Matrix to categorize tasks into four quadrants: important and urgent, important but not urgent, urgent but not important, and not urgent or important.

Create a To-Do List: Make a daily or weekly to-do list to keep track of your tasksBreak down larger tasks into smaller, more manageable steps.

Use Time Management Techniques: Use techniques like the Pomodoro Technique, where you work for a set amount of time (e.g., 25 minutes) and then take a short break (e.g., 5 minutes)This can help improve focus and productivity.

Delegate and Outsource: Learn to delegate tasks that can be done by othersThis will free up your time to focus on more important tasksIf possible, consider outsourcing tasks that are not within your expertise.

Use Technology Tools: Take advantage of technology tools like task management apps, project management software, and calendar apps to help you stay organized and manage your tasks effectively.

Break Tasks into Smaller Steps: Breaking down larger tasks into smaller, more manageable steps can make them less overwhelming and easier to tackle.

Set Deadlines: Set realistic deadlines for your tasks and projectsThis will help you stay focused and ensure that you complete your work on time.

Minimize Distractions: Identify and minimize distractions that can hinder your productivityThis may include turning off notifications on your phone, closing unnecessary tabs on your computer, or finding a quiet workspace.

Review and Reflect: Regularly review your progress and reflect on what is working and what needs improvementMake adjustments to your planning and organization techniques as needed.

Remember, everyone has their own preferred techniques, so feel free to experiment and find what works best for you.

11- Using Technology to Enhance Time Management

Technology has become an integral part of our lives, and it can be a powerful tool for enhancing time management. Here are some ways in which technology can help us better manage our time:

Calendar and scheduling apps: Utilizing calendar and scheduling apps can help us organize our time effectively. These apps allow us to schedule appointments, set reminders, and create to-do lists, ensuring that we stay on track and meet our deadlines.

Task management tools: Task management tools such as Trello, Asana, or Todoist can help us prioritize and manage our tasks efficientlyThese tools enable us to create task lists, set due dates, and track our progress, ensuring that we stay focused and complete our tasks on time.

Time tracking apps: Time tracking apps can help us monitor how we spend our time and identify areas where we can improve our productivityThese apps allow us to track the time spent on different activities, set goals, and analyze our time usage patterns, enabling us to make necessary adjustments to optimize our time management.

Communication and collaboration tools: Technology has revolutionized communication and collaboration, making it easier for teams to work together efficientlyTools like Slack, Microsoft Teams, or Google Workspace provide instant messaging, video conferencing, and document sharing capabilities, allowing teams to communicate and collaborate in real-time, saving time and enhancing productivity.

Automation tools: Automation tools can help us automate repetitive tasks, freeing up our time for more important activitiesFor example, email filters can automatically sort and prioritize incoming emails, saving us time and reducing distractionsSimilarly, automation tools like IFTTT or Zapier can integrate different apps and automate workflows, streamlining our processes.

Time management apps: There are various time management apps available that can help us track and analyze how we spend our timeThese apps provide insights into our daily habits, identify time-wasting activities, and suggest ways to improve our time management skills.

In conclusion, technology offers numerous tools and applications that can greatly enhance our time management abilities. By utilizing these tools effectively, we can optimize our productivity, meet deadlines, and achieve a better work-life balance.

12- Managing Email and Digital Communication

Managing email and digital communication is essential for staying organized and efficient in today's digital age. Here are some tips to help you effectively manage your email and digital communication:

Set specific times for checking and responding to emails: Instead of constantly checking your inbox throughout the day, allocate specific times to check and respond to emails. This will help you stay focused on other tasks and avoid getting overwhelmed by a constant stream of incoming messages.

Use email filters and folders: Set up filters and folders in your email client to automatically sort incoming emails into different categories or foldersThis can help you prioritize and organize your emails based on their importance or topic.

Unsubscribe from unnecessary email subscriptions: Take the time to unsubscribe from email newsletters and subscriptions that you no longer find useful or relevantThis will help declutter your inbox and reduce the amount of incoming emails.

Use email templates and canned responses: If you find yourself frequently sending similar emails or responses, consider creating email templates or canned responsesThis can save you time and effort when composing repetitive emails.

Prioritize and flag important emails: Identify and prioritize emails that require immediate attention or actionUse flags or labels to mark these emails so that you can easily find and address them later.

Use a task management system: If your email client supports it, use a task management system to create and track tasks related to your emailsThis can help you stay organized and ensure that important emails are not forgotten or overlooked.

Avoid multitasking: When responding to emails, try to focus on one task at a timeAvoid multitasking as it can lead to errors and decrease productivityFinish one email before moving on to the next.

Be concise and clear in your emails: Keep your emails brief and to the pointUse clear and concise language to convey your message effectivelyThis will help ensure that your emails are read and understood by the recipients.

Use email signatures: Create a professional email signature that includes your contact information and any relevant links or social media profilesThis can save you time when sending emails and provide recipients with the necessary information to contact you.

Take breaks from digital communication: It's important to take regular breaks from digital communication to avoid burnoutDisconnect from your email and other digital platforms during non-working hours to recharge and maintain a healthy work-life balance.

By following these tips, you can effectively manage your email and digital communication, leading to increased productivity and reduced stress.

13- Strategies for Effective Decision Making

Effective decision making is a crucial skill in both personal and professional life. Here are some strategies that can help improve decision-making:

Define the problem: Clearly identify the problem or decision that needs to be made. This will help you focus your efforts and avoid wasting time on irrelevant factors.

Gather information: Collect all relevant information and data related to the decisionThis may involve conducting research, consulting experts, or analyzing past experiences.

Analyze the options: Evaluate the available options and consider their potential outcomesUse techniques such as cost-benefit analysis, SWOT analysis, or decision matrices to compare and prioritize the options.

Consider the consequences: Think about the potential consequences of each optionConsider both short-term and long-term impacts, as well as the potential risks and benefits.

Involve others: Seek input and perspectives from others who may have valuable insights or expertiseThis can help you gain a broader understanding of the situation and consider alternative viewpoints.

Trust your intuition: While data and analysis are important, don't ignore your gut feelings or intuitionSometimes, your instincts can provide valuable insights that data alone may not capture.

Evaluate and decide: Assess the pros and cons of each option and make a decision based on the information and analysisConsider the feasibility, practicality, and alignment with your goals and values.

Take action: Implement your decision and take the necessary steps to put it into actionMonitor the results and be prepared to adapt or revise your decision if needed.

Learn from the outcomes: Reflect on the outcomes of your decision and learn from both successes and failuresUse this knowledge to improve your decision-making skills in the future.

Remember, effective decision making is a skill that can be developed and improved over time. By following these strategies and continuously learning from your experiences, you can become a more effective decision maker.

14- Delegating Tasks and Responsibilities

Delegating tasks and responsibilities is an important skill for effective management and teamwork. Here are some key steps to follow when delegating tasks:

Identify the task: Start by clearly identifying the task or responsibility that needs to be delegated. Consider the specific skills, knowledge, and experience required to complete the task successfully.

Select the right person: Choose the most suitable person or team to delegate the task toConsider their abilities, workload, and availabilityEnsure that they have the necessary skills and resources to complete the task effectively.

Communicate expectations: Clearly communicate the expectations and objectives of the task to the person or team you are delegating toProvide them with all the necessary information, resources, and guidelines to ensure they understand what needs to be done.

Provide support: Offer support and guidance to the person or team you have delegated the task toBe available to answer questions, provide clarification, and offer assistance whenever neededThis will help them feel supported and confident in their ability to complete the task.

Set deadlines: Establish clear deadlines for the completion of the taskMake sure the deadlines are realistic and achievableRegularly check in with the person or team to monitor progress and provide feedback.

Trust and empower: Trust the person or team you have delegated the task to and empower them to make decisions and take ownership of the taskAvoid micromanaging and allow them to use their skills and creativity to complete the task in their own way.

Monitor and evaluate: Continuously monitor the progress of the delegated task and evaluate the resultsProvide feedback and recognition for a job well doneIf necessary, offer additional support or make adjustments to ensure the successful completion of the task.

Remember, effective delegation not only helps distribute workload but also develops the skills and capabilities of your team members. It promotes collaboration, improves productivity, and allows you to focus on higher-level tasks and responsibilities.

15-Effective Time Blocking Techniques

Sure! Here are some effective time blocking techniques:

Prioritize tasks: Start by listing down all the tasks you need to accomplish. Then, prioritize them based on their importance and urgency.

Set specific time blocks: Allocate specific time blocks for different types of tasksFor example, you can have a block for emails, a block for meetings, a block for focused work, etc.

Avoid multitasking: Instead of trying to do multiple tasks at once, focus on one task during each time blockThis helps improve concentration and productivity.

Break tasks into smaller chunks: If you have a large task, break it down into smaller, more manageable chunksThis makes it easier to allocate time for each part and prevents overwhelm.

Schedule breaks: Don't forget to schedule short breaks in between time blocksTaking regular breaks can help refresh your mind and prevent burnout.

Be flexible: While time blocking helps in organizing your day, it's important to be flexible and adapt to unexpected changes or interruptions that may arise.

Use a digital or physical planner: Choose a planner that works best for you, whether it's a digital calendar or a physical plannerUse it to schedule and track your time blocks.

Review and adjust: At the end of each day or week, review how well you stuck to your time blocks and make adjustments as neededThis helps in refining your time management skills.

Remember, the key to effective time blocking is to be disciplined and consistent with your schedule. It may take some time to find the right balance, but with practice, you can improve your productivity and achieve your goals.

16- Managing Meetings and Appointments

Managing meetings and appointments is an essential task for effective time management and collaboration. Here are some tips to help you manage your meetings and appointments efficiently:

Use a calendar or scheduling tool: Utilize a digital calendar or scheduling tool to keep track of all your meetings and appointments. This will help you stay organized and avoid double bookings.

Set clear objectives: Before scheduling a meeting, define the purpose and objectivesThis will ensure that everyone attending the meeting understands its importance and can come prepared.

Share an agenda: Share a meeting agenda with all participants before the meetingThis will help them prepare and contribute effectively during the meeting.

Schedule buffer time: Leave some buffer time between meetings to allow for breaks, follow-up actions, or unexpected delaysThis will prevent back-to-back meetings and give you time to regroup.

Send reminders: Send meeting reminders to all participants a day or a few hours before the scheduled meetingThis will help ensure that everyone is aware of the meeting and can attend on time.

Take meeting notes: During the meeting, take notes to capture important points, decisions, and action itemsShare these notes with the participants after the meeting for reference.

Follow up on action items: After the meeting, follow up on the action items assigned to each participantSet deadlines and track progress to ensure that tasks are completed on time.

Evaluate meeting effectiveness: Periodically evaluate the effectiveness of your meetingsSolicit feedback from participants and make necessary adjustments to improve future meetings.

By following these tips, you can effectively manage your meetings and appointments, leading to better productivity and collaboration.

17- Strategies for Efficient Workflows

Efficient workflows are crucial for productivity and ensuring tasks are completed in a timely manner. Here are some strategies to help you improve your workflow efficiency:

Prioritize tasks: Start by identifying the most important and urgent tasks. Prioritize them based on their deadlines and importance to ensure you focus on the right things at the right time.

Break tasks into smaller steps: Large tasks can be overwhelming and lead to procrastinationBreak them down into smaller, more manageable stepsThis will make it easier to stay focused and track your progress.

Use task management tools: Utilize task management tools such as Trello, Asana, or Todoist to organize and track your tasksThese tools allow you to create to-do lists, set deadlines, and collaborate with team members.

Eliminate distractions: Minimize distractions by turning off notifications on your phone, closing unnecessary tabs on your computer, and creating a dedicated workspaceThis will help you stay focused and complete tasks more efficiently.

Delegate tasks: If possible, delegate tasks that can be done by othersThis will free up your time to focus on more important or complex tasksDelegating also promotes teamwork and allows others to develop their skills.

Use automation tools: Take advantage of automation tools to streamline repetitive tasksFor example, you can use email filters to automatically sort and prioritize incoming emails, or use project management software to automate task assignments and reminders.

Time blocking: Allocate specific time blocks for different types of tasksThis helps you stay organized and ensures that you dedicate enough time to each task without getting overwhelmed.

Take regular breaks: Breaks are essential for maintaining focus and preventing burnoutSchedule short breaks throughout the day to recharge and refresh your mindUse techniques like the Pomodoro

Technique, where you work for a set amount of time and then take a short break.

Continuous learning: Invest time in learning new skills and tools that can improve your workflow efficiencyStay updated with the latest trends and technologies in your field to find better ways of doing things.

Reflect and optimize: Regularly review your workflow and identify areas for improvementReflect on what worked well and what didn't, and make adjustments accordinglyContinuous optimization is key to maintaining an efficient workflow.

By implementing these strategies, you can enhance your workflow efficiency and accomplish more in less time. Remember, finding the right workflow that suits your needs may require some experimentation and adjustments along the way.

18- Managing Work-Life Balance

Managing work-life balance is crucial for maintaining overall well-being and productivity. Here are some tips to help you achieve a healthy work-life balance:

Set boundaries: Establish clear boundaries between work and personal life. Define specific working hours and avoid bringing work-related tasks into your personal time.

Prioritize tasks: Identify your most important tasks and focus on completing them firstThis will help you manage your time effectively and prevent work from spilling over into your personal life.

Delegate and outsource: Learn to delegate tasks that can be handled by othersIf possible, consider outsourcing certain responsibilities to free up your time and reduce stress.

Take regular breaks: Schedule regular breaks throughout the day to recharge and relaxUse this time to engage in activities that help you unwind and rejuvenate.

Practice self-care: Make self-care a priorityEngage in activities that promote physical and mental well-being, such as exercise, meditation, or hobbies that you enjoy.

Communicate with your employer: If you are feeling overwhelmed with work, have an open and honest conversation with your employerDiscuss your workload and explore potential solutions to achieve a better work-life balance.

Disconnect from technology: Set boundaries with technology by limiting your use of electronic devices during your personal timeAvoid checking work emails or messages outside of working hours.

Plan and organize: Plan your schedule in advance and organize your tasks effectivelyThis will help you stay on track and avoid last-minute stress.

Set realistic expectations: Be realistic about what you can accomplish within a given timeframeAvoid overcommitting yourself and learn to say no when necessary.

Seek support: Reach out to friends, family, or colleagues for support when neededHaving a strong support system can help you navigate challenges and maintain a healthy work-life balance.

Remember, achieving work-life balance is an ongoing process that requires conscious effort and prioritization. By implementing these tips, you can create a more harmonious and fulfilling life.

19- Strategies for Effective Time Tracking

Effective time tracking is crucial for maximizing productivity and managing tasks efficiently. Here are some strategies to help you improve your time tracking:

Set Clear Goals: Start by defining your goals and priorities for each day or week. This will give you a clear direction and help you allocate your time effectively.

Use Time Tracking Tools: Utilize time tracking tools and apps to monitor and record your time spent on different tasksThese tools can provide valuable insights into your productivity patterns and help you identify areas for improvement.

Break Down Tasks: Break down larger tasks into smaller, more manageable sub-tasksThis will make it easier to estimate the time required for each task and track your progress accurately.

Prioritize Important Tasks: Identify the most important and urgent tasks and prioritize them accordinglyBy focusing on high-priority tasks first, you can ensure that your time is allocated to the most critical activities.

Minimize Distractions: Create a distraction-free work environment by eliminating or minimizing distractions such as phone notifications, social media, and unnecessary meetingsThis will help you stay focused and make better use of your time.

Schedule Regular Breaks: Taking regular breaks is essential for maintaining productivity and preventing burnoutUse time tracking tools to schedule short breaks throughout the day, allowing yourself time to recharge and refocus.

Review and Analyze: Regularly review your time tracking data to analyze your productivity and identify areas for improvementLook for patterns, bottlenecks, and time-wasting activities that can be eliminated or optimized.

Adjust and Adapt: Be flexible and willing to adjust your time tracking strategies as neededExperiment with different techniques and approaches to find what works best for you and your workflow.

By implementing these strategies, you can enhance your time tracking practices and improve your overall productivity and efficiency. Remember, effective time tracking is a continuous process that requires regular monitoring and adjustment to ensure optimal results.

20-Overcoming Time Management Challenges

To overcome time management challenges, here are some strategies you can try:

Prioritize tasks: Start by identifying the most important tasks that need to be done. Focus on completing these tasks first before moving on to less important ones.

Set goals: Set clear and achievable goals for each day, week, or monthThis will help you stay focused and motivated to complete your tasks on time.

Create a schedule: Plan your day in advance by creating a scheduleAllocate specific time slots for different tasks and activitiesBe realistic about how much time each task will take.

Avoid multitasking: Multitasking can lead to decreased productivity and increased stressInstead, focus on one task at a time and give it your full attention.

Delegate tasks: If possible, delegate tasks to othersThis will free up your time to focus on more important tasks or activities.

Minimize distractions: Identify and minimize distractions that can eat up your timeThis can include turning off notifications on your phone, closing unnecessary tabs on your computer, or finding a quiet place to work.

Take regular breaks: Taking short breaks throughout the day can actually improve your productivityUse these breaks to relax, stretch, or do something enjoyable.

Learn to say no: It's important to learn to say no to tasks or activities that are not aligned with your priorities or goalsThis will help you avoid overcommitting yourself and feeling overwhelmed.

Use technology tools: Take advantage of time management tools and apps that can help you stay organized and track your progressThese can include to-do list apps, calendar apps, or project management tools.

Practice self-care: Taking care of yourself is essential for effective time managementMake sure to get enough sleep, eat well, exercise regularly, and engage in activities that help you relax and recharge.

Remember, overcoming time management challenges takes practice and consistency. Find the strategies that work best for you and make them a part of your daily routine.

21- Developing Healthy Habits for Time Management

Developing healthy habits for time management is essential for maintaining productivity and reducing stress. Here are some tips to help you develop these habits:

Set Clear Goals: Start by setting clear and specific goals for each day, week, and month. This will help you prioritize your tasks and stay focused on what needs to be done.

Prioritize Tasks: Once you have your goals set, prioritize your tasks based on their importance and urgencyFocus on completing high-priority tasks first before moving on to less important ones.

Create a Schedule: Develop a daily or weekly schedule that includes dedicated time slots for different activities and tasksThis will help you allocate time effectively and avoid wasting time on unproductive activities.

Avoid Procrastination: Procrastination can be a major time wasterTry to identify the reasons behind your procrastination and find ways to overcome itBreak tasks into smaller, manageable chunks and set deadlines to stay motivated.

Practice Time Blocking: Time blocking involves dedicating specific blocks of time to specific tasks or activitiesThis helps you stay focused and prevents distractions from interrupting your work.

Take Regular Breaks: It's important to take regular breaks to rest and rechargeSchedule short breaks throughout the day to relax and rejuvenateThis will help maintain your energy and focus.

Delegate and Outsource: Learn to delegate tasks that can be done by others and outsource tasks that are not within your expertiseThis will free up your time to focus on more important and high-value activities.

Avoid Multitasking: Multitasking may seem efficient, but it often leads to decreased productivity and increased errorsInstead, focus on one task at a time and give it your full attention.

Learn to Say No: It's important to set boundaries and learn to say no to tasks or commitments that are not aligned with your goals or prioritiesThis will help you avoid overcommitting and spreading yourself too thin.

Reflect and Adjust: Regularly reflect on your time management habits and adjust them as neededIdentify what is working well and what needs improvement, and make necessary changes to optimize your productivity.

Remember, developing healthy habits for time management takes time and practice. Be patient with yourself and stay committed to implementing these habits consistently.

22- Strategies for Effective Task Management

Strategies for Effective Task Management

Task management is an essential skill that helps individuals and teams stay organized, focused, and productive. Effective task management involves planning, prioritizing, and executing tasks in a systematic and efficient manner. In this essay, we will explore various strategies for effective task management.

One of the key strategies for effective task management is proper planning. Before starting any task, it is important to have a clear understanding of the objectives, requirements, and deadlines. By creating a detailed plan, individuals can break down complex tasks into smaller, more manageable steps. This allows for better time management and ensures that all necessary resources are available.

Prioritization is another crucial aspect of effective task management. Not all tasks are created equal, and it is important to identify and focus on the most important and urgent ones. The Eisenhower Matrix is a popular tool that can help individuals prioritize tasks based on their importance and urgency. By categorizing tasks into four quadrants - important and urgent, important but not urgent, urgent but not important, and not urgent and not important - individuals can allocate their time and energy more effectively.

In addition to planning and prioritization, effective task management also requires effective execution. This involves breaking down tasks into smaller, actionable steps and setting realistic deadlines for each step. By setting specific and achievable goals, individuals can stay motivated and track their progress. It is also important to eliminate distractions and create a conducive work environment to maintain focus and productivity.

Another strategy for effective task management is delegation. Recognizing that one person cannot do everything, delegating tasks to others can help distribute the workload and ensure that tasks are completed in a timely manner. Delegation also allows individuals to leverage the strengths and expertise of others, leading to better outcomes.

Furthermore, effective task management involves regular review and adjustment. It is important to periodically review the progress of tasks and make necessary adjustments to the plan. This allows individuals to stay flexible and adapt to changing circumstances. By reflecting on past experiences and learning from mistakes, individuals can continuously improve their task management skills.

In conclusion, effective task management is crucial for individuals and teams to stay organized, focused, and productive. By implementing strategies such as proper planning, prioritization, effective execution, delegation, and regular review, individuals can enhance their task management skills and achieve better outcomes. Developing these strategies and incorporating them into daily routines can lead to increased efficiency and success in both personal and professional endeavors.

23- Managing Time in a Team Environment

Managing Time in a Team Environment

Time management is a crucial skill in any team environment. When working collaboratively, it is essential to effectively manage time to ensure productivity, meet deadlines, and achieve goals. In this essay, we will explore the importance of managing time in a team environment and discuss strategies for improving time management skills.

One of the primary reasons why time management is crucial in a team environment is that it helps to maintain productivity. When team members effectively manage their time, they can allocate sufficient time to each task, ensuring that all tasks are completed efficiently. This not only enhances individual productivity but also contributes to the overall success of the team. By managing time effectively, team members can avoid procrastination and stay focused on their responsibilities.

Meeting deadlines is another significant aspect of managing time in a team environment. In a collaborative setting, team members often rely on each other's work to complete their own tasks. If one team member fails to manage their time effectively and misses a deadline, it can have a domino effect on the entire team's progress. Therefore, by managing time efficiently, team members can ensure that they meet deadlines and maintain a smooth workflow.

Effective time management also plays a crucial role in achieving team goals. When team members are aware of their individual responsibilities and manage their time accordingly, they can contribute to the overall progress of the team. By setting realistic deadlines and allocating time for each task, team members can work towards achieving the team's objectives in a systematic and organized manner.

To improve time management skills in a team environment, several strategies can be implemented. Firstly, it is essential to prioritize tasks based on their importance and urgency. By identifying the most critical tasks and allocating time accordingly, team members can ensure that they focus on the most significant aspects of their work.

Another effective strategy is to break down complex tasks into smaller, manageable subtasks. By dividing a large task into smaller parts, team members can approach the work in a more systematic and organized manner. This not only helps in managing time effectively but also reduces the feeling of overwhelm and improves productivity.

Furthermore, effective communication within the team is vital for managing time efficiently. By regularly updating each other on the progress of tasks and discussing any challenges or roadblocks, team members can collectively work towards finding solutions and ensuring that the project stays on track. Clear communication helps in avoiding misunderstandings, delays, and unnecessary rework.

In conclusion, managing time in a team environment is crucial for maintaining productivity, meeting deadlines, and achieving team goals. By implementing strategies such as prioritizing tasks, breaking down complex tasks, and fostering effective communication, team members can improve their time management skills and contribute to the success of the team. Effective time management not only benefits individual team members but also enhances the overall efficiency and effectiveness of the team.

24-Strategies for Effective Time Estimation

Effective time estimation is a crucial skill that can greatly impact our productivity and success in various aspects of life. Whether it's completing a project, meeting a deadline, or managing daily tasks, having the ability to accurately estimate the time required is essential. In this essay, we will explore some strategies for effective time estimation and how they can be applied in different situations.

One of the key strategies for effective time estimation is breaking down tasks into smaller, more manageable chunks. When faced with a complex task, it can be overwhelming to estimate the time required for its completion. However, by breaking it down into smaller subtasks, we can gain a better understanding of the individual components and estimate their time requirements more accurately. This approach also allows us to identify any potential bottlenecks or dependencies that may affect the overall time estimation.

Another important strategy is considering past experiences and data. Reflecting on similar tasks or projects that we have completed in the past can provide valuable insights into the time required for similar future endeavors. By analyzing the time it took to complete similar tasks and considering any challenges or obstacles encountered, we can make more informed estimates for future projects. Additionally, keeping a record of our time spent on different activities can help us identify patterns and improve our estimation skills over time.

Furthermore, it is essential to account for unexpected delays and interruptions when estimating time. No matter how well we plan, unforeseen circumstances can arise and disrupt our workflow. By factoring in some buffer time for these unexpected events, we can mitigate the impact of delays and ensure that our time estimation remains realistic. This approach also helps us maintain a sense of flexibility and adaptability in our schedules.

In addition to the strategies mentioned above, effective communication and collaboration with others can significantly improve time estimation. When working on a team or collaborating with others, it is important to consider different perspectives and gather input from all stakeholders. By involving others in the estimation process, we can benefit from their expertise and insights, leading to more accurate time estimates. Moreover, effective communication ensures that everyone is on the same page regarding project timelines and deadlines, reducing the likelihood of misunderstandings or delays.

Lastly, it is crucial to regularly review and adjust our time estimation strategies. Time estimation is not a one-time task; it requires continuous improvement and refinement. By reflecting on our past estimations and analyzing any discrepancies between the estimated and actual time taken, we can identify areas for improvement and adjust our strategies accordingly. This iterative process helps us become more proficient in time estimation and enhances our overall productivity.

In conclusion, effective time estimation is a skill that can greatly enhance our productivity and success. By employing strategies such as breaking down tasks, considering past experiences, accounting for unexpected delays, collaborating with others, and regularly reviewing and adjusting our strategies, we can improve our time estimation skills. With practice and experience, we can become more accurate in estimating the time required for various tasks and projects, leading to better planning and successful outcomes.

25-Managing Time during Travel and Commuting

Managing time during travel and commuting can be challenging, but with some effective strategies, you can make the most of your time. Here are a few tips to help you manage your time effectively:

Plan Ahead: Before you start your journey, plan your route and schedule. This will help you allocate time for different activities and ensure that you are prepared for any unexpected delays.

Use Travel Time Productively: Make use of your travel time by engaging in activities that can be done on the goFor example, you can listen to audiobooks, podcasts, or language lessons, or catch up on emails and work tasks.

Prioritize Tasks: Identify the most important tasks that need to be completed during your travel timeFocus on those tasks first to ensure that you make progress on your work or personal projects.

Make Use of Technology: Take advantage of technology tools and apps that can help you stay organized and productive during your commuteFor example, you can use productivity apps to manage your tasks, set reminders, and track your progress.

Break Tasks into Smaller Chunks: If you have larger tasks to complete, break them down into smaller, more manageable chunksThis will help you make progress even during short periods of time.

Stay Focused: Minimize distractions during your travel time by creating a conducive environmentFor example, you can use noise-canceling headphones to block out noise or find a quiet spot to work.

Use Offline Mode: If you are traveling in an area with limited or no internet connectivity, download necessary files, documents, or entertainment in advanceThis will ensure that you can continue working or stay entertained even without an internet connection.

Take Breaks: It's important to give yourself short breaks during your travel time to relax and rechargeUse this time to stretch, meditate, or simply take a few deep breaths.

Remember, managing time during travel and commuting is all about being proactive and making the most of the available time. By implementing these strategies, you can make your travel time more productive and enjoyable.

26-Strategies for Effective Project Management

Strategies for Effective Project Management

Project management is a crucial aspect of any organization's success. It involves planning, organizing, and controlling resources to achieve specific goals within a defined timeframe. To ensure the successful completion of a project, it is essential to employ effective strategies. In this essay, we will explore some key strategies for effective project management.

Clear Project Objectives: The first step in effective project management is to establish clear and measurable project objectives. These objectives should be specific, realistic, and achievable. By clearly defining the project's goals, the project manager can align the team's efforts towards a common purpose.

Detailed Planning: A well-defined project plan is essential for effective project managementThis plan should outline the project's scope, deliverables, timelines, and resource requirementsIt should also include a breakdown of tasks and responsibilities, allowing for better coordination and accountability.

Effective Communication: Communication plays a vital role in project managementIt is crucial to establish open and transparent channels of communication among team members, stakeholders, and clientsRegular status updates, meetings, and progress reports help ensure that everyone is on the same page and aware of any changes or challenges.

Risk Management: Identifying and managing risks is an integral part of project managementA comprehensive risk management plan should be developed to identify potential risks, assess their impact, and define mitigation strategiesBy proactively addressing risks, project managers can minimize their impact on project timelines and deliverables.

Resource Allocation: Efficient resource allocation is essential for effective project managementProject managers need to identify the necessary resources, such as personnel, equipment, and budget, and allocate them appropriatelyThis ensures that the project has the required resources at each stage, preventing delays and bottlenecks.

Stakeholder Engagement: Engaging stakeholders throughout the project lifecycle is crucial for its successProject managers should involve key stakeholders in decision-making processes, seek their input, and address their concernsThis fosters a sense of ownership and commitment, leading to better project outcomes.

Continuous Monitoring and Evaluation: Regular monitoring and evaluation are essential to track the project's progress and identify any deviations from the planProject managers should establish key performance indicators (KPIs) and use them to measure the project's successThis allows for timely adjustments and corrective actions to keep the project on track.

Adaptability and Flexibility: Projects often encounter unexpected challenges and changesEffective project management requires adaptability and flexibility to respond to these changes promptlyProject managers should be prepared to revise plans, reallocate resources, and adjust timelines as needed to ensure project success.

In conclusion, effective project management is crucial for the successful completion of any project. By employing strategies such as clear project objectives, detailed planning, effective communication, risk management, resource allocation, stakeholder engagement, continuous monitoring and evaluation, and adaptability, project managers can increase the likelihood of achieving project goals. These strategies help ensure that projects are delivered on time, within budget, and meet the desired quality standards.

27- Managing Time in a Remote Work Environment

Managing Time in a Remote Work Environment

In recent years, remote work has become increasingly popular, allowing individuals to work from the comfort of their own homes or any location of their choice. While remote work offers numerous benefits, such as flexibility and increased productivity, it also presents unique challenges, particularly when it comes to managing time effectively. In this essay, we will explore the importance of managing time in a remote work environment and discuss strategies to enhance productivity and maintain a healthy work-life balance.

One of the key challenges of remote work is the blurred line between work and personal life. Without the physical separation of a traditional office, it can be difficult to establish boundaries and maintain a structured schedule. As a result, individuals may find themselves working longer hours or struggling to switch off from work-related tasks. To address this issue, it is crucial to establish a clear daily routine and set specific working hours. By defining a start and end time for work, individuals can create a sense of structure and ensure that they allocate time for personal activities and relaxation.

Another important aspect of managing time in a remote work environment is prioritization. With the absence of direct supervision and constant distractions, it is easy to lose focus and get overwhelmed by the multitude of tasks at hand. To overcome this challenge, individuals should develop effective prioritization techniques, such as creating to-do lists, setting deadlines, and breaking down complex tasks into smaller, more manageable steps. By identifying the most important and urgent tasks, individuals can allocate their time and energy accordingly, ensuring that they meet deadlines and achieve their goals.

Furthermore, effective time management in a remote work environment requires the use of technology and digital tools. With the abundance of productivity apps, project management software, and communication platforms available, individuals can leverage these tools to streamline their workflow, collaborate with team members, and track their progress. For instance, project management tools like Trello or Asana can help individuals organize their tasks and monitor their progress, while communication platforms like Slack or Microsoft Teams facilitate seamless collaboration and communication with colleagues. By utilizing these tools, individuals can optimize their time and enhance their productivity.

In addition to utilizing technology, it is essential to create a conducive work environment that promotes focus and minimizes distractions. Remote work often means working from home, where there may be various distractions, such as household chores, family members, or personal devices. To combat these distractions, individuals should designate a specific workspace that is free from distractions and establish boundaries with family members or roommates. Additionally, practicing good time management habits, such as taking regular breaks, setting aside time for exercise or relaxation, and avoiding multitasking, can help individuals maintain focus and productivity throughout the day.

Lastly, maintaining a healthy work-life balance is crucial for long-term success in a remote work environment. It is easy to fall into the trap of working excessively, especially when there is no physical separation between work and personal life. However, overworking can lead to burnout, decreased productivity, and negatively impact one's mental and physical well-being. To avoid this, individuals should prioritize self-care and allocate time for activities outside of work, such as hobbies, spending time with loved ones, or pursuing personal interests. By setting boundaries and making time for non-work-related activities, individuals can achieve a better work-life balance and sustain their productivity in the long run.

In conclusion, managing time effectively in a remote work environment is crucial for maintaining productivity, achieving goals, and ensuring a healthy work-life balance. By establishing a structured routine, prioritizing tasks, utilizing technology and digital tools, creating a conducive work environment, and maintaining a healthy work-life balance, individuals can overcome the challenges of remote work and thrive in their professional and personal lives. With proper time management, remote work can be a rewarding and fulfilling experience.

28- Strategies for Effective Time Management for Students

Effective time management is crucial for students to succeed academically and maintain a healthy work-life balance. With numerous assignments, exams, extracurricular activities, and personal commitments, students often find themselves overwhelmed and struggling to manage their time effectively. However, by implementing certain strategies, students can optimize their time and achieve their goals. This essay will discuss some effective strategies for time management for students.

One of the most important strategies for effective time management is setting clear goals and priorities. Students should identify their short-term and long-term goals and prioritize their tasks accordingly. By doing so, they can allocate their time and energy to the most important tasks and avoid wasting time on less significant activities. Setting specific, measurable, achievable, relevant, and time-bound (SMART) goals can provide students with a clear roadmap and help them stay focused.

Another crucial strategy is creating a schedule or a timetable. Students should allocate specific time slots for studying, attending classes, completing assignments, and engaging in extracurricular activities. By creating a structured schedule, students can ensure that they dedicate sufficient time to each task and avoid procrastination. It is important to be realistic while creating a schedule and allow for breaks and leisure activities to prevent burnout.

Furthermore, effective time management requires students to eliminate distractions. In today's digital age, distractions such as social media, online games, and smartphones can easily consume a significant amount of time. Students should develop the discipline to minimize or eliminate these distractions during study hours. They can use productivity apps or website blockers to limit their access to distracting websites and focus on their tasks.

In addition, students should learn to effectively prioritize and delegate tasks. Not all tasks require the same level of attention and effort. By identifying tasks that can be delegated to others or tasks that are less important, students can free up their time for more critical activities. Learning to say no to non-essential commitments can also help students manage their time more effectively.

Moreover, effective time management involves taking regular breaks and practicing self-care. Students should recognize the importance of rest and relaxation in maintaining productivity and overall well-being. Taking short breaks during study sessions can help improve focus and prevent mental fatigue. Engaging in physical activities, practicing mindfulness, and getting enough sleep are also essential for optimal time management.

Lastly, students should regularly evaluate and adjust their time management strategies. What works for one student may not work for another, so it is important to reflect on one's own habits and make necessary adjustments. By analyzing their productivity levels and identifying areas for improvement, students can refine their time management skills and achieve better results.

In conclusion, effective time management is crucial for students to succeed academically and maintain a balanced lifestyle. By setting clear goals, creating a schedule, eliminating distractions, prioritizing tasks, taking breaks, and regularly evaluating their strategies, students can optimize their time and achieve their goals. Implementing these strategies will not only improve academic performance but also enhance overall well-being.

29- Managing Time for Personal Growth and Development

Managing Time for Personal Growth and Development

Time is a valuable resource that, if managed effectively, can lead to personal growth and development. In today's fast-paced world, it is crucial to prioritize and allocate time wisely to achieve our goals and aspirations. This essay will explore the importance of managing time for personal growth and development and provide practical strategies to enhance time management skills.

One of the key benefits of managing time effectively is the ability to focus on personal growth. When we allocate specific time slots for activities that contribute to our personal development, such as learning new skills, pursuing hobbies, or engaging in self-reflection, we create opportunities for self-improvement. By dedicating time to these activities, we can enhance our knowledge, broaden our perspectives, and develop new talents, ultimately leading to personal growth.

Furthermore, effective time management allows individuals to set and achieve goals. By setting clear objectives and breaking them down into smaller, manageable tasks, we can create a roadmap for success. By allocating time for each task and adhering to a schedule, we can make progress towards our goals and experience a sense of accomplishment. This not only boosts our self-confidence but also motivates us to continue striving for personal growth and development.

In addition, managing time well enables individuals to maintain a healthy work-life balance. By allocating time for work, leisure, relationships, and self-care, we can ensure that all aspects of our lives are given the attention they deserve. This balance is crucial for overall well-being and personal growth. When we have time for relaxation and rejuvenation, we can recharge our energy and approach tasks with a fresh perspective. This, in turn, enhances our productivity and allows us to make the most of our time.

To effectively manage time for personal growth and development, it is essential to employ practical strategies. Firstly, individuals should prioritize tasks based on their importance and urgency. By identifying the most critical tasks and allocating time for them, we can ensure that our time is spent on activities that align with our goals. Additionally, individuals should learn to delegate tasks when possible, allowing them to focus on activities that contribute directly to personal growth. Moreover, setting realistic deadlines and breaking tasks into smaller, manageable chunks can help prevent procrastination and ensure progress is made consistently.

Another useful strategy is to eliminate time-wasting activities and distractions. This may involve reducing time spent on social media, limiting screen time, or creating a dedicated workspace free from distractions. By minimizing distractions,

30-Strategies for Effective Time Management for Entrepreneurs

Time management is a crucial skill for entrepreneurs to master in order to maximize productivity and achieve their goals. With the numerous responsibilities and demands that come with running a business, effective time management strategies are essential for entrepreneurs to stay organized, focused, and efficient. In this essay, we will explore some key strategies that entrepreneurs can employ to effectively manage their time.

One of the most important strategies for effective time management is setting clear goals and priorities. Entrepreneurs should have a clear understanding of their long-term objectives and break them down into smaller, actionable tasks. By prioritizing these tasks based on their importance and urgency, entrepreneurs can allocate their time and resources effectively. This helps them stay focused on the most critical tasks and avoid wasting time on less important activities.

Another strategy for effective time management is creating a schedule or a daily plan. Entrepreneurs should allocate specific time slots for different activities, such as meetings, client calls, administrative tasks, and personal time. By having a structured schedule, entrepreneurs can ensure that they are dedicating sufficient time to each task and avoiding unnecessary distractions. It is also important to build in buffer time for unexpected events or emergencies that may arise.

Delegation is another key strategy that entrepreneurs can utilize to manage their time effectively. As a business owner, it is important to recognize that you cannot do everything on your own. Delegating tasks to capable team members or outsourcing certain activities can free up valuable time for entrepreneurs to focus on more important aspects of their business. This not only helps in managing time but also allows entrepreneurs to leverage the skills and expertise of others, leading to better outcomes.

In addition to delegation, entrepreneurs should also learn to say no. It is common for entrepreneurs to be approached with various opportunities, requests, or invitations. While it may be tempting to say yes to everything, it is important to evaluate the potential impact on time and resources. By saying no to non-essential tasks or commitments, entrepreneurs can protect their time and ensure that they are dedicating their efforts to activities that align with their goals and priorities.

Furthermore, entrepreneurs should embrace technology and utilize productivity tools to streamline their workflow. There are numerous time management apps, project management software, and communication tools available that can help entrepreneurs stay organized, collaborate efficiently with team members, and track progress on tasks. By leveraging these tools, entrepreneurs can automate repetitive tasks, reduce manual effort, and improve overall productivity.

Lastly, entrepreneurs should prioritize self-care and personal well-being. It is easy for entrepreneurs to get caught up in the demands of their business and neglect their own physical and mental health. However, taking care of oneself is crucial for long-term success. Entrepreneurs should make time for exercise, relaxation, hobbies, and spending quality time with loved ones. By maintaining a healthy work-life balance, entrepreneurs can recharge, reduce stress, and ultimately perform better in their business endeavors.

In conclusion, effective time management is essential for entrepreneurs to succeed in their business ventures. By setting clear goals and priorities, creating a schedule, delegating tasks, learning to say no, utilizing technology, and prioritizing self-care, entrepreneurs can optimize their time and achieve greater productivity. With these strategies in place, entrepreneurs can navigate the challenges of running a business more efficiently and effectively.

31- Managing Time for Health and Well-being

Managing Time for Health and Well-being

Time management is a crucial skill that plays a significant role in maintaining our health and well-being. In today's fast-paced world, where we are constantly bombarded with numerous responsibilities and commitments, it is essential to effectively manage our time to ensure a balanced and fulfilling life. This essay explores the importance of managing time for health and well-being and provides practical tips on how to achieve this.

One of the key benefits of managing time for health and well-being is the reduction of stress. When we effectively allocate our time to different activities, we can avoid the feeling of being overwhelmed and rushed. By creating a schedule that includes time for work, exercise, relaxation, and socializing, we can maintain a healthy balance in our lives. This balance allows us to better cope with stress and prevents burnout, ultimately improving our overall well-being.

Furthermore, managing time for health and well-being enables us to prioritize self-care. In our busy lives, it is easy to neglect our own needs and focus solely on meeting the demands of others. However, by consciously setting aside time for activities that promote our physical and mental well-being, such as exercise, meditation, and hobbies, we can enhance our overall quality of life. Taking care of ourselves not only improves our health but also increases our productivity and ability to handle challenges effectively.

In addition, effective time management allows us to cultivate healthy habits. When we allocate time for regular exercise, meal planning, and adequate sleep, we establish a routine that supports our physical health. These habits contribute to increased energy levels, improved focus, and a strengthened immune system. By making time for these essential activities, we invest in our long-term well-being and reduce the risk of developing chronic illnesses.

Moreover, managing time for health and well-being fosters better relationships. When we prioritize spending quality time with loved ones, we strengthen our bonds and create a support system that enhances our emotional well-being. By setting boundaries and allocating time for socializing, we can nurture our relationships and prevent feelings of isolation or loneliness. Strong social connections have been proven to have a positive impact on mental health and overall life satisfaction.

To effectively manage time for health and well-being, it is important to implement practical strategies. Firstly, it is crucial to set clear goals and prioritize tasks based on their importance and urgency. By identifying our priorities, we can allocate time accordingly and avoid wasting valuable time on less important activities. Secondly, creating a schedule or using time management tools can help us stay organized and ensure that we allocate sufficient time for different activities. Thirdly, learning to say no and setting boundaries is essential to avoid overcommitting ourselves and feeling overwhelmed. Lastly, it is important to regularly evaluate our time management strategies and make adjustments as needed to maintain a healthy balance.

In conclusion, managing time for health and well-being is essential in today's fast-paced world. By effectively allocating our time, we can reduce stress, prioritize self-care, cultivate healthy habits, and foster better relationships. Implementing practical strategies such as goal setting, scheduling, setting boundaries, and regular evaluation can help us achieve a balanced and fulfilling life. By making time for our health and well-being, we invest in ourselves and ultimately lead happier and more satisfying lives.

32- Strategies for Effective Time Management for Parents

Effective time management is crucial for parents who are juggling multiple responsibilities and trying to balance work, household chores, and quality time with their children. In this essay, we will explore strategies that can help parents effectively manage their time and create a harmonious balance in their lives.

One of the key strategies for effective time management for parents is prioritization. Parents need to identify their most important tasks and allocate time accordingly. This involves setting clear goals and determining which activities are essential and which can be delegated or eliminated. By prioritizing tasks, parents can focus on what truly matters and avoid wasting time on less important activities.

Another important strategy is creating a schedule or a routine. Establishing a daily or weekly schedule can help parents stay organized and ensure that they allocate time for each task or responsibility. This can include setting specific times for work, household chores, and spending quality time with children. By following a schedule, parents can avoid procrastination and make the most of their available time.

Additionally, effective time management for parents involves learning to say no. It is important for parents to recognize their limits and not overcommit themselves. Saying no to additional responsibilities or social engagements that do not align with their priorities can help parents avoid feeling overwhelmed and ensure that they have enough time for their core responsibilities and their children.

Furthermore, parents can benefit from utilizing technology and tools to streamline their tasks and save time. There are numerous apps and software available that can help parents manage their schedules, create to-do lists, and set reminders. By leveraging these tools, parents can automate certain tasks and free up time for more important activities.

In addition to these strategies, effective communication and delegation are crucial for parents to manage their time effectively. Parents should communicate their needs and expectations with their partners, family members, or caregivers, and delegate tasks whenever possible. Sharing responsibilities can help lighten the load and create more time for parents to focus on their children and other important aspects of their lives.

Lastly, self-care is an essential component of effective time management for parents. Taking care of one's physical and mental well-being is crucial for maintaining productivity and managing stress. Parents should prioritize self-care activities such as exercise, relaxation, and pursuing hobbies, as these can help recharge their energy and improve overall time management.

In conclusion, effective time management is essential for parents to maintain a healthy work-life balance and ensure quality time with their children. By prioritizing tasks, creating schedules, learning to say no, utilizing technology, communicating effectively, and practicing self-care, parents can optimize their time and create a more fulfilling and balanced life.

33- Managing Time for Creative Pursuits

Managing Time for Creative Pursuits

Time management is a crucial skill for individuals engaged in creative pursuits. Whether it's writing, painting, or any other form of artistic expression, effectively managing time can greatly enhance productivity and creativity. In this essay, we will explore the importance of time management for creative individuals and discuss some strategies to optimize time for creative pursuits.

One of the main challenges that creative individuals face is finding the time to engage in their artistic endeavors. With busy schedules and numerous responsibilities, it can be difficult to carve out dedicated time for creative pursuits. However, by prioritizing and managing time effectively, it is possible to create a conducive environment for creativity to flourish.

One strategy for managing time for creative pursuits is setting specific goals and deadlines. By establishing clear objectives, creative individuals can allocate their time more efficiently. For example, a writer may set a goal of writing a certain number of pages or completing a chapter within a specific timeframe. This not only provides a sense of direction but also helps in breaking down the creative process into manageable tasks.

Another important aspect of time management for creative individuals is creating a routine. Having a consistent schedule helps in establishing a rhythm and allows for better focus and concentration. By designating specific time slots for creative activities, individuals can train their minds to be more productive during those periods. This routine can also help in overcoming creative blocks and maintaining a consistent level of motivation.

In addition to setting goals and establishing a routine, it is essential to eliminate distractions and create a conducive environment for creativity. This may involve turning off notifications on electronic devices, finding a quiet space to work, or using tools that help in staying focused. By minimizing distractions, creative individuals can make the most of their time and channel their energy towards their artistic pursuits.

Furthermore, time management for creative individuals also involves taking breaks and allowing for rest and rejuvenation. While it may seem counterintuitive, taking regular breaks can actually enhance productivity and creativity. Stepping away from the creative process for a short period allows the mind to relax and recharge, leading to fresh perspectives and new ideas.

In conclusion, managing time effectively is crucial for individuals engaged in creative pursuits. By setting goals, establishing a routine, eliminating distractions, and allowing for rest, creative individuals can optimize their time and enhance their productivity and creativity. Time management is not only about allocating time for creative activities but also about creating a conducive environment that nurtures and supports artistic expression. With proper time management, individuals can unlock their creative potential and achieve their artistic goals.

34- Strategies for Effective Time Management for Seniors

Effective time management is crucial for seniors who want to make the most out of their golden years. As we age, our time becomes even more valuable, and it is essential to prioritize and manage our activities efficiently. In this essay, we will explore some strategies for effective time management for seniors.

First and foremost, seniors should create a daily or weekly schedule to plan their activities. By having a clear plan, seniors can allocate their time to different tasks and ensure that they are making progress towards their goals. This schedule should include not only essential tasks such as appointments and errands but also activities that bring joy and fulfillment, such as hobbies or spending time with loved ones.

Another important strategy for effective time management is setting realistic goals. Seniors should identify their priorities and focus on activities that align with their values and interests. By setting achievable goals, seniors can avoid feeling overwhelmed and maintain a sense of accomplishment. It is also essential to break down larger tasks into smaller, manageable steps to make progress consistently.

Seniors should also learn to delegate tasks and ask for help when needed. As we age, it is natural to experience physical limitations or health issues that may make certain tasks more challenging. By delegating tasks to family members, friends, or hired professionals, seniors can free up their time and energy for activities that bring them joy and fulfillment. It is important for seniors to recognize that asking for help is not a sign of weakness but rather a smart strategy for effective time management.

Furthermore, seniors should prioritize self-care and relaxation. Taking care of one's physical and mental well-being is crucial for overall productivity and happiness. Seniors should make time for activities such as exercise, meditation, or pursuing hobbies that promote relaxation and reduce stress. By prioritizing self-care, seniors can maintain their energy levels and improve their ability to manage their time effectively.

Lastly, seniors should embrace technology and utilize digital tools to streamline their tasks and stay organized. There are numerous apps and software available that can help seniors manage their schedules, set reminders, and track their progress. By leveraging technology, seniors can save time and reduce the risk of forgetting important tasks or appointments.

In conclusion, effective time management is essential for seniors to make the most out of their golden years. By creating a schedule, setting realistic goals, delegating tasks, prioritizing self-care, and utilizing technology, seniors can optimize their time and focus on activities that bring them joy and fulfillment. With proper time management, seniors can lead a balanced and fulfilling life in their senior years.

35- Managing Time for Continuous Learning

Managing Time for Continuous Learning

Time management is a crucial skill for individuals who strive for continuous learning. In today's fast-paced world, where information is readily available and new knowledge is constantly being generated, effectively managing time becomes essential to ensure that one can keep up with the ever-evolving landscape of knowledge and skills. This essay will explore the importance of managing time for continuous learning and provide practical strategies to enhance time management in the pursuit of lifelong learning.

One of the primary reasons why managing time is crucial for continuous learning is the limited nature of time itself. Each day consists of only 24 hours, and how we allocate and utilize this time greatly impacts our ability to engage in learning activities. Without proper time management, it becomes easy to get overwhelmed and fall behind in acquiring new knowledge and skills. Therefore, individuals who prioritize continuous learning must develop effective strategies to make the most of their available time.

One practical strategy for managing time for continuous learning is setting clear goals and priorities. By identifying specific learning objectives and prioritizing them based on their importance and urgency, individuals can allocate their time more efficiently. This involves breaking down larger learning goals into smaller, manageable tasks and creating a schedule or to-do list to ensure that each task is given the necessary attention and time. By having a clear roadmap of what needs to be accomplished, individuals can stay focused and avoid wasting time on less important activities.

Another important aspect of time management for continuous learning is minimizing distractions. In today's digital age, distractions are abundant, with social media, emails, and other notifications constantly vying for our attention. To effectively manage time for learning, it is essential to create a conducive environment that minimizes distractions. This can be achieved by turning off notifications, setting specific times for checking emails and social media, and creating a dedicated workspace free from distractions. By eliminating or reducing distractions, individuals can maximize their concentration and productivity during their learning sessions.

Furthermore, effective time management for continuous learning involves adopting efficient learning techniques. Not all learning methods are created equal, and some techniques can help individuals learn more effectively in less time. For example, techniques such as spaced repetition, active recall, and chunking can enhance learning efficiency and retention. By incorporating these techniques into their study routine, individuals can optimize their learning process and make the most of their available time.

Lastly, it is important to recognize the value of breaks and rest in time management for continuous learning. While it may seem counterintuitive, taking regular breaks can actually improve productivity and learning outcomes. Studies have shown that our brains need time to rest and consolidate information for effective learning. Therefore, individuals should schedule short breaks during their learning sessions to recharge and rejuvenate their minds. Additionally, ensuring an adequate amount of sleep is crucial for optimal cognitive function and learning. By prioritizing rest and incorporating breaks into their study schedule, individuals can maintain their focus and productivity over the long term.

In conclusion, managing time effectively is essential for continuous learning. By setting clear goals and priorities, minimizing distractions, adopting efficient learning techniques, and recognizing the importance of breaks and rest, individuals can optimize their time for learning. Continuous learning is a lifelong journey, and by developing strong time management skills, individuals can ensure that they make the most of their available time and stay ahead in their pursuit of knowledge and personal growth.

36- Strategies for Effective Time Management for Sales Professionals

Effective time management is crucial for sales professionals to maximize their productivity and achieve their sales targets. In today's fast-paced business environment, sales professionals often face numerous tasks and responsibilities that require careful planning and organization. By implementing effective time management strategies, sales professionals can prioritize their activities, minimize distractions, and optimize their productivity. This essay will discuss some essential strategies for effective time management for sales professionals.

One of the most important strategies for effective time management is setting clear goals and priorities. Sales professionals should identify their key objectives and break them down into smaller, manageable tasks. By prioritizing tasks based on their importance and urgency, sales professionals can focus their time and energy on activities that directly contribute to their sales targets. This approach helps them avoid wasting time on non-essential tasks and ensures that they are consistently working towards their goals.

Another crucial strategy for effective time management is creating a schedule or daily plan. Sales professionals should allocate specific time slots for different activities, such as prospecting, client meetings, follow-ups, and administrative tasks. By having a structured schedule, sales professionals can better manage their time and avoid overloading themselves with multiple tasks at once. It is also important to allocate time for breaks and relaxation to prevent burnout and maintain productivity throughout the day.

Utilizing technology and automation tools is another effective time management strategy for sales professionals. There are various software applications and tools available that can streamline sales processes, automate repetitive tasks, and provide valuable insights. For example, customer relationship management (CRM) software can help sales professionals track leads, manage customer data, and streamline communication. By leveraging technology, sales professionals can save time on manual tasks and focus on building relationships and closing deals.

Effective communication and delegation are also essential for effective time management. Sales professionals should prioritize effective communication with their team members, managers, and clients. Clear and concise communication helps avoid misunderstandings, delays, and unnecessary back-and-forth. Additionally, sales professionals should delegate tasks that can be handled by others, allowing them to focus on high-value activities that require their expertise. Delegation not only saves time but also empowers team members and fosters collaboration.

Furthermore, sales professionals should practice effective time-blocking techniques. Time blocking involves dedicating specific blocks of time to specific tasks or activities. This technique helps sales professionals stay focused and avoid distractions. By setting aside uninterrupted time for important tasks, sales professionals can maximize their productivity and accomplish more in less time. It is important to communicate to colleagues and team members about these time blocks to minimize interruptions and ensure a productive work environment.

Lastly, sales professionals should regularly evaluate and adjust their time management strategies. It is important to reflect on what is working and what needs improvement. By analyzing their time usage, sales professionals can identify areas of inefficiency and make necessary adjustments. This could involve eliminating time-wasting activities, optimizing workflows, or seeking additional training and support. Continuous improvement is key to maintaining effective time management practices.

In conclusion, effective time management is essential for sales professionals to succeed in their roles. By setting clear goals, creating a schedule, utilizing technology, practicing effective communication and delegation, implementing time-blocking techniques, and regularly evaluating and adjusting strategies, sales professionals can optimize their productivity and achieve their sales targets. With effective time management, sales professionals can effectively balance their workload, increase efficiency, and ultimately drive success in their sales endeavors.

37- Managing Time for Effective Networking

Managing Time for Effective Networking

Networking plays a crucial role in today's professional world. It allows individuals to connect with others, build relationships, and create opportunities for personal and career growth. However, managing time effectively is essential to make the most out of networking efforts. In this essay, we will explore the importance of time management in networking and provide practical tips for maximizing networking opportunities.

Time management is the process of planning and organizing one's time to achieve specific goals and objectives. When it comes to networking, effective time management is crucial because it allows individuals to allocate their time wisely and focus on activities that yield the greatest results. Here are some reasons why managing time is essential for effective networking:

Prioritization: Time management helps individuals prioritize their networking activities. By identifying the most important networking events, meetings, or opportunities, individuals can allocate their time accordingly. This ensures that they invest their time in activities that align with their goals and have the potential to yield significant benefits.

Efficiency: Effective time management enables individuals to be more efficient in their networking effortsBy planning ahead and organizing their schedule, individuals can avoid wasting time on unproductive activities or events that do not contribute to their networking goalsThis allows them to focus on building meaningful connections and making the most out of each networking opportunity.

Follow-up: Networking is not just about attending events or meeting new people; it also involves nurturing and maintaining relationshipsTime management plays a crucial role in following up with contacts and staying connectedBy setting aside dedicated time for follow-up activities, individuals can ensure that they stay engaged with their network and build stronger relationships over time.

Now that we understand the importance of time management in networking, let's explore some practical tips for managing time effectively:

Set clear goals: Before diving into networking activities, it is essential to set clear goals and objectives. By defining what you want to achieve through networking, you can prioritize your time and focus on activities that align with your goals.

Plan ahead: Take the time to plan your networking activities in advanceThis includes identifying relevant events, scheduling meetings, and allocating time for follow-up activitiesBy planning ahead, you can ensure that you make the most out of each networking opportunity.

Use technology: Leverage technology tools to streamline your networking effortsUse calendar apps to schedule events and meetings, use contact management systems to organize your network, and utilize social media platforms to stay connected with contactsTechnology can help you save time and stay organized.

Be selective: Not every networking opportunity will be equally valuableBe selective in choosing which events or meetings to attendFocus on quality rather than quantity and prioritize opportunities that align with your goals and interests.

Delegate and outsource: If possible, delegate or outsource tasks that are not directly related to networkingThis could include administrative tasks, event logistics, or follow-up activitiesBy delegating non-essential tasks, you can free up more time to focus on building relationships and making meaningful connections.

In conclusion, effective time management is crucial for successful networking. By prioritizing, being efficient, and dedicating time for follow-up activities, individuals can make the most out of their networking efforts. By setting clear goals, planning ahead, leveraging technology, being selective, and delegating tasks, individuals can manage their time effectively and maximize networking opportunities. Remember, networking is not just about meeting new people; it is about building relationships and creating opportunities for personal and career growth.

38- Strategies for Effective Time Management for Freelancers

Strategies for Effective Time Management for Freelancers

Time management is crucial for freelancers who work independently and manage their own schedules. Without proper time management, freelancers may struggle to meet deadlines, experience burnout, and have difficulty maintaining a healthy work-life balance. To ensure productivity and success, freelancers should implement effective time management strategies. In this essay, we will explore some strategies that can help freelancers effectively manage their time.

Set Clear Goals and Prioritize Tasks: Freelancers should start by setting clear goals for their work. By defining what needs to be accomplished, freelancers can prioritize tasks accordingly. Breaking down larger projects into smaller, manageable tasks can make them less overwhelming and easier to tackle. Prioritizing tasks based on their importance and urgency can help freelancers stay focused and ensure that they complete their work on time.

Create a Schedule: Establishing a schedule is essential for freelancers to manage their time effectivelyBy creating a daily or weekly schedule, freelancers can allocate specific time slots for different tasks and activitiesThis helps in maintaining a structured routine and prevents procrastinationIt is important to consider individual productivity patterns and energy levels when creating a scheduleAllocating time for breaks and relaxation is equally important to avoid burnout.

Use Time-Tracking Tools: Freelancers can benefit from using time-tracking tools to monitor their work hours and track the time spent on different tasksThese tools provide insights into how time is being utilized and help identify areas where improvements can be madeTime-tracking tools also help freelancers stay accountable and ensure that they are dedicating enough time to their work.

Avoid Multitasking: While multitasking may seem like a way to get more done in less time, it often leads to decreased productivity and quality of workFreelancers should focus on one task at a time and give it their full attentionBy avoiding multitasking, freelancers can complete tasks more efficiently and produce higher-quality work.

Set Realistic Deadlines: Setting realistic deadlines is crucial for effective time managementFreelancers should evaluate the scope of work and their own capabilities before committing to deadlinesOvercommitting can lead to stress and compromised quality of workSetting realistic deadlines allows freelancers to manage their workload effectively and deliver high-quality work within the agreed-upon timeframe.

Minimize Distractions: Distractions can significantly impact productivity and time managementFreelancers should identify common distractions in their work environment and take steps to minimize themThis may involve turning off notifications on electronic devices, creating a dedicated workspace, or using productivity apps that block distracting websites or apps during work hours.

Practice Self-Care: Taking care of one's physical and mental well-being is essential for effective time managementFreelancers should prioritize self-care activities such as exercise, proper nutrition, and sufficient sleepEngaging in activities that help reduce stress and promote relaxation, such as meditation or hobbies, can also contribute to better time management by improving focus and overall well-being.

In conclusion, effective time management is crucial for freelancers to succeed in their work. By setting clear goals, creating a schedule, using time-tracking tools, avoiding multitasking, setting realistic deadlines, minimizing distractions, and practicing self-care, freelancers can optimize their productivity, meet deadlines, and maintain a healthy work-life balance. Implementing these strategies will not only enhance time management skills but also contribute to overall professional growth and success as a freelancer.

111

39- Managing Time for Volunteer Work and Community Involvement

Managing Time for Volunteer Work and Community Involvement
Volunteer work and community involvement play a crucial role in creating a positive impact on society. However, managing time effectively for these activities can be challenging. In this essay, we will explore the importance of managing time for volunteer work and community involvement, as well as provide practical tips for doing so.

Firstly, managing time for volunteer work and community involvement is essential because it allows individuals to contribute to causes they care about. Many people have a strong desire to make a difference in their communities, but without proper time management, it can be difficult to find the time to get involved. By effectively managing their time, individuals can allocate specific hours or days to engage in volunteer work or community activities, ensuring that they can actively contribute to the causes they are passionate about.

Secondly, managing time for volunteer work and community involvement helps individuals maintain a healthy work-life balance. In today's fast-paced world, it is easy to become overwhelmed with work and personal commitments, leaving little time for community engagement. However, by prioritizing and managing time effectively, individuals can create a balance between their professional and personal lives, allowing them to dedicate time to volunteer work and community involvement without neglecting other important aspects of their lives.

To effectively manage time for volunteer work and community involvement, individuals can follow several practical tips. Firstly, it is essential to prioritize activities and commitments. By identifying the most important volunteer work or community activities, individuals can allocate their time accordingly. This may involve assessing the impact of each activity and determining which ones align with their values and goals.

Additionally, individuals can create a schedule or calendar to plan their time effectively. By setting aside specific time slots for volunteer work and community involvement, individuals can ensure that they have dedicated time for these activities. This can also help in avoiding conflicts with other commitments and responsibilities.

Furthermore, individuals should learn to delegate tasks and ask for help when needed. Volunteer work and community involvement often require teamwork, and by delegating tasks to others or seeking assistance, individuals can reduce their workload and ensure that tasks are completed efficiently. This can also create opportunities for collaboration and shared responsibility within the community.

Lastly, individuals should practice self-care and avoid overcommitting themselves. It is important to recognize personal limits and not take on more than one can handle. By maintaining a healthy balance between volunteer work, community involvement, and personal well-being, individuals can sustain their commitment and make a long-term impact.

In conclusion, managing time for volunteer work and community involvement is crucial for individuals who wish to contribute to causes they care about and maintain a healthy work-life balance. By prioritizing, planning, delegating, and practicing self-care, individuals can effectively manage their time and actively engage in volunteer work and community activities. Through these efforts, individuals can make a positive difference in their communities and inspire others to get involved as well.

40- Strategies for Effective Time Management for Busy Professionals

Effective time management is crucial for busy professionals who are constantly juggling multiple responsibilities and tasks. It allows them to maximize productivity, reduce stress, and achieve a better work-life balance. In this essay, we will explore some strategies that can help busy professionals effectively manage their time.

One of the most important strategies for effective time management is prioritization. Busy professionals often have a long list of tasks and deadlines to meet. By prioritizing tasks based on their importance and urgency, professionals can ensure that they focus their time and energy on the most critical activities. This can be done by creating a to-do list and categorizing tasks into different levels of priority. By tackling high-priority tasks first, professionals can make progress on important projects and avoid last-minute rushes.

Another strategy for effective time management is setting realistic goals and deadlines. Busy professionals often face tight deadlines and high expectations. However, it is important to set realistic goals and deadlines that can be achieved without compromising the quality of work. By breaking down big projects into smaller, manageable tasks and setting realistic timelines for each task, professionals can avoid feeling overwhelmed and ensure that they stay on track.

Furthermore, effective time management involves avoiding multitasking. While multitasking may seem like a way to get more done in less time, it often leads to decreased productivity and increased errors. Busy professionals should focus on one task at a time and give it their full attention. This allows them to work more efficiently and produce higher-quality results. By eliminating distractions and creating a dedicated work environment, professionals can minimize interruptions and stay focused on the task at hand.

In addition, effective time management requires effective delegation. Busy professionals cannot do everything themselves, and it is important to recognize when tasks can be delegated to others. Delegating tasks not only frees up time for professionals to focus on more important responsibilities but also allows others to develop their skills and contribute to the team. By assigning tasks to the right people and providing clear instructions, professionals can ensure that work is completed efficiently and effectively.

Lastly, effective time management involves taking breaks and practicing self-care. Busy professionals often neglect their own well-being in the pursuit of productivity. However, taking regular breaks and engaging in activities that promote relaxation and rejuvenation is essential for maintaining focus and avoiding burnout. Whether it's going for a walk, practicing mindfulness, or spending time with loved ones, professionals should prioritize self-care as part of their time management strategy.

In conclusion, effective time management is crucial for busy professionals to thrive in their demanding roles. By prioritizing tasks, setting realistic goals, avoiding multitasking, delegating effectively, and practicing self-care, professionals can optimize their productivity, reduce stress, and achieve a better work-life balance. Implementing these strategies can lead to increased efficiency, improved job satisfaction, and overall success in both personal and professional endeavors.

41- Managing Time for Personal Relationships

Managing Time for Personal Relationships

Time is a precious resource that we all have in limited supply. In today's fast-paced world, it can be challenging to find the time to nurture and maintain personal relationships. However, managing time effectively is crucial for the well-being of our relationships and overall happiness. In this essay, we will explore the importance of managing time for personal relationships and discuss some strategies to achieve a healthy balance.

First and foremost, personal relationships require time and attention to thrive. Whether it is with our partners, family members, or close friends, investing time in these relationships is essential for building trust, understanding, and connection. Neglecting personal relationships due to a lack of time can lead to feelings of loneliness, isolation, and even relationship breakdowns. Therefore, it is crucial to prioritize and allocate time for our loved ones.

One effective strategy for managing time for personal relationships is to establish clear boundaries and set aside dedicated time for them. This can be done by creating a schedule or a routine that includes specific times for spending quality time with loved ones. By setting aside uninterrupted time, we can fully engage in meaningful conversations, activities, and shared experiences. It is important to communicate these boundaries to others and ensure that they are respected.

Another important aspect of managing time for personal relationships is learning to say no to non-essential commitments. Often, we find ourselves overwhelmed with various obligations and responsibilities, leaving little time for personal relationships. It is crucial to evaluate our priorities and determine what truly matters to us. By saying no to unnecessary commitments, we can free up time to invest in our personal relationships and create a healthier work-life balance.

Furthermore, technology has become an integral part of our lives, and it can both help and hinder our ability to manage time for personal relationships. While technology allows us to stay connected with others, it can also be a major distraction. It is important to set boundaries with technology and limit its use during dedicated personal time. By disconnecting from screens and focusing on the present moment, we can strengthen our relationships and deepen our connections with others.

In addition to setting boundaries and saying no, effective time management techniques can also contribute to managing time for personal relationships. Prioritizing tasks, delegating responsibilities, and practicing efficient work habits can help create more free time for personal interactions. By being organized and disciplined with our time, we can strike a balance between work, personal commitments, and relationships.

In conclusion, managing time for personal relationships is essential for maintaining healthy and fulfilling connections with our loved ones. By establishing clear boundaries, saying no to non-essential commitments, setting aside dedicated time, and practicing effective time management techniques, we can ensure that our personal relationships receive the attention and care they deserve. Remember, time is a valuable resource, and investing it in our relationships is a worthwhile endeavor that brings joy, love, and fulfillment into our lives.

42- Strategies for Effective Time Management for Teachers

Effective time management is crucial for teachers to ensure they can fulfill their responsibilities and provide quality education to their students. With numerous tasks to juggle, such as lesson planning, grading, meetings, and extracurricular activities, teachers need to employ strategies that help them make the most of their time. In this essay, we will explore some effective strategies for time management that teachers can implement to enhance their productivity and maintain a healthy work-life balance.

One of the key strategies for effective time management is prioritization. Teachers should identify their most important tasks and allocate time accordingly. By focusing on high-priority tasks first, teachers can ensure that critical responsibilities are fulfilled without delay. This can be achieved by creating a to-do list or using a digital task management tool to organize and prioritize tasks based on urgency and importance.

Another important aspect of time management for teachers is effective planning. Teachers should allocate specific time slots for different activities, such as lesson planning, grading, and administrative tasks. By creating a schedule and sticking to it, teachers can avoid wasting time and ensure that all tasks are completed within the allocated time frame. Additionally, teachers should consider incorporating buffer time in their schedule to account for unexpected interruptions or emergencies.

Furthermore, teachers can benefit from utilizing technology to streamline their tasks and save time. There are various digital tools and applications available that can assist teachers in managing their time more efficiently. For example, online grading platforms can automate the grading process, reducing the time spent on manual grading. Additionally, digital lesson planning tools can help teachers organize and store lesson materials, making it easier to access and reuse them in the future.

Collaboration and delegation are also effective strategies for time management. Teachers can collaborate with their colleagues to share resources, lesson plans, and teaching strategies. By working together, teachers can save time and enhance the quality of their teaching. Furthermore, teachers should not hesitate to delegate tasks to their students or teacher assistants when appropriate. Delegating tasks such as setting up classroom materials or organizing files can free up valuable time for teachers to focus on more important responsibilities.

In addition to these strategies, it is essential for teachers to practice self-care and maintain a healthy work-life balance. Taking breaks, engaging in hobbies, and spending time with loved ones are crucial for recharging and avoiding burnout. By prioritizing self-care, teachers can improve their overall well-being and productivity.

In conclusion, effective time management is vital for teachers to fulfill their responsibilities and provide quality education. By implementing strategies such as prioritization, effective planning, utilizing technology, collaboration, delegation, and practicing self-care, teachers can enhance their productivity, maintain a healthy work-life balance, and ultimately create a positive learning environment for their students. It is important for teachers to continuously evaluate and adjust their time management strategies to ensure they are maximizing their efficiency and effectiveness in the classroom.

43- Managing Time for Personal Finances

Managing Time for Personal Finances

Time management is a crucial skill that can greatly impact our personal finances. Effectively managing our time allows us to allocate the necessary time and attention to various financial tasks, such as budgeting, saving, investing, and paying bills. In this essay, we will explore the importance of managing time for personal finances and discuss some strategies to improve time management in this area.

One of the key aspects of managing time for personal finances is creating and sticking to a budget. A budget helps us track our income and expenses, allowing us to make informed decisions about how we spend and save our money. However, creating a budget requires time and effort. We need to gather information about our income sources, fixed expenses, variable expenses, and financial goals. By allocating dedicated time to review and update our budget regularly, we can ensure that we are on track with our financial plans.

Another important aspect of time management for personal finances is saving and investing. Saving money is essential for building an emergency fund, achieving financial goals, and preparing for retirement. It is crucial to set aside time to evaluate our saving goals, research different saving options, and regularly contribute to our savings accounts. Similarly, investing requires time for research, monitoring the market, and managing our investment portfolio. By dedicating time to educate ourselves about different investment options and regularly reviewing our investments, we can make informed decisions to grow our wealth.

Paying bills on time is another critical aspect of managing time for personal finances. Late payments can result in additional fees, penalties, and damage to our credit score. To avoid these consequences, it is important to allocate time to review and pay our bills promptly. Setting up automatic payments or creating reminders can help us stay organized and ensure that we meet all our financial obligations on time.

In addition to these specific tasks, managing time for personal finances also involves developing good financial habits. This includes regularly reviewing our financial statements, tracking our expenses, and staying informed about financial news and trends. By dedicating time to these activities, we can identify any potential issues, make necessary adjustments, and stay proactive in managing our finances.

To improve time management for personal finances, it can be helpful to prioritize financial tasks and set specific goals. By identifying the most important financial tasks and allocating time for them, we can ensure that we focus on what matters most. Additionally, setting specific goals can provide motivation and help us stay on track. Breaking down larger financial goals into smaller, manageable tasks can make them more achievable and less overwhelming.

In conclusion, managing time for personal finances is crucial for achieving financial stability and success. By effectively managing our time, we can create and stick to a budget, save and invest wisely, pay bills on time, and develop good financial habits. Prioritizing financial tasks and setting specific goals can help us improve our time management in this area. Ultimately, by dedicating time and attention to our personal finances, we can build a solid foundation for a secure and prosperous financial future.

44- Strategies for Effective Time Management for Writers

Strategies for Effective Time Management for Writers

Time management is a crucial skill for writers to master in order to maximize productivity and achieve their writing goals. With the demands of daily life and the numerous distractions that can derail focus, implementing effective time management strategies is essential. Here are some strategies that writers can employ to make the most of their time:

Set Clear Goals: Before starting any writing task, it is important to establish clear goals. This could be completing a certain number of pages, finishing a chapter, or meeting a specific word count. By setting clear goals, writers can prioritize their tasks and allocate their time accordingly.

Create a Schedule: Developing a schedule is a fundamental aspect of effective time managementWriters should create a daily or weekly schedule that outlines specific writing timesThis schedule should also include breaks and time for other commitmentsBy adhering to a schedule, writers can establish a routine and ensure that they dedicate sufficient time to their writing.

Eliminate Distractions: Distractions can significantly hinder productivityWriters should identify and eliminate distractions that may disrupt their writing processThis could involve turning off notifications on electronic devices, finding a quiet workspace, or using productivity apps that block certain websites or applications during writing sessions.

Prioritize Tasks: Not all writing tasks are created equalIt is important for writers to prioritize their tasks based on importance and urgencyBy focusing on high-priority tasks first, writers can ensure that they allocate their time effectively and complete the most critical work first.

Break Tasks into Manageable Chunks: Writing projects can often feel overwhelming, especially when facing tight deadlinesBreaking tasks into smaller, manageable chunks can make them more approachableWriters can divide their work into sections or set specific milestones to track progress and maintain motivation.

Use Time-Blocking Techniques: Time-blocking is a technique where writers allocate specific blocks of time for different tasksBy assigning dedicated time slots for writing, editing, research, and other activities, writers can maintain focus and prevent tasks from overlapping or taking longer than necessary.

Take Regular Breaks: While it may seem counterintuitive, taking regular breaks is essential for maintaining productivityWriters should incorporate short breaks into their schedule to rest, recharge, and prevent burnoutThese breaks can help clear the mind and enhance creativity when returning to the writing process.

Practice Self-Care: Writers must prioritize self-care to maintain their overall well-being and productivityThis includes getting enough sleep, eating nutritious meals, exercising regularly, and engaging in activities that provide relaxation and rejuvenationTaking care of oneself physically and mentally is crucial for optimal time management.

Seek Accountability: Holding oneself accountable can be challenging, especially when working independentlyWriters can seek accountability by joining writing groups, participating in writing challenges, or finding a writing buddyBy sharing progress and goals with others, writers can stay motivated and committed to their writing schedule.

Reflect and Adjust: Time management strategies are not one-size-fits-allIt is important for writers to regularly reflect on their progress and adjust their strategies as neededThis could involve evaluating the effectiveness of certain techniques, identifying areas for improvement, and making necessary changes to optimize time management.

In conclusion, effective time management is essential for writers to maximize productivity and achieve their writing goals. By setting clear goals, creating a schedule, eliminating distractions, prioritizing tasks, breaking tasks into manageable chunks, using time-blocking techniques, taking regular breaks, practicing self-care, seeking accountability, and reflecting and adjusting, writers can optimize their time and make significant progress in their writing endeavors. With dedication and consistent implementation of these strategies, writers can overcome challenges and enhance their overall writing experience.

45-Managing Time for Self-Care and Relaxation

Managing Time for Self-Care and Relaxation

In today's fast-paced world, it is easy to get caught up in the hustle and bustle of daily life. With work, family, and other responsibilities, it can feel like there is never enough time in the day. However, it is crucial to prioritize self-care and relaxation to maintain a healthy and balanced lifestyle. Managing time effectively is key to achieving this goal.

One of the first steps in managing time for self-care and relaxation is to recognize its importance. Many people mistakenly believe that taking time for themselves is selfish or unproductive. However, self-care is essential for physical, mental, and emotional well-being. It allows individuals to recharge, reduce stress, and improve overall productivity. By understanding the benefits of self-care, individuals can prioritize it in their daily lives.

Next, it is important to set boundaries and establish a routine. This includes allocating specific time slots for self-care activities such as exercise, meditation, hobbies, or simply relaxing. By creating a schedule and sticking to it, individuals can ensure that they have dedicated time for themselves. It is also crucial to communicate these boundaries to others, whether it be family, friends, or colleagues, to avoid unnecessary interruptions or conflicts.

Another effective strategy for managing time for self-care and relaxation is to practice time management techniques. This involves prioritizing tasks, setting realistic goals, and avoiding procrastination. By efficiently managing time, individuals can create more opportunities for self-care activities. This may include delegating tasks, breaking larger tasks into smaller, manageable ones, and utilizing tools such as calendars or to-do lists to stay organized.

Additionally, it is important to learn to say no. Many individuals struggle with saying no to additional responsibilities or commitments, fearing that they may disappoint others. However, constantly overextending oneself can lead to burnout and neglect of personal needs. By setting boundaries and learning to decline requests that do not align with one's priorities, individuals can create more time for self-care and relaxation.

Furthermore, technology can both help and hinder time management for self-care. While technology provides convenience and efficiency, it can also be a major source of distraction and time-wasting. It is important to establish healthy boundaries with technology, such as setting designated screen-free times or limiting social media usage. By minimizing distractions, individuals can make the most of their time for self-care and relaxation.

Lastly, it is crucial to be flexible and adaptable in managing time for self-care and relaxation. Life is unpredictable, and unexpected events or responsibilities may arise. It is important to be able to adjust schedules and priorities accordingly without feeling guilty or overwhelmed. By practicing self-compassion and understanding that self-care is a priority, individuals can navigate through these challenges while still making time for themselves.

In conclusion, managing time for self-care and relaxation is essential for maintaining a healthy and balanced lifestyle. By recognizing the importance of self-care, setting boundaries, practicing time management techniques, learning to say no, establishing healthy technology habits, and being flexible, individuals can create more opportunities for self-care and relaxation. Remember, taking care of oneself is not selfish but rather a necessary investment in overall well-being.

46- Strategies for Effective Time Management for Managers

Effective time management is crucial for managers to ensure productivity and success in their roles. Managers are responsible for overseeing multiple tasks, projects, and teams, making it essential for them to have effective strategies in place to manage their time efficiently. In this essay, we will explore some strategies that managers can adopt to enhance their time management skills.

One of the key strategies for effective time management is setting clear goals and priorities. Managers should identify their most important tasks and prioritize them based on their urgency and importance. By focusing on high-priority tasks, managers can allocate their time and resources effectively, ensuring that critical objectives are met. Setting clear goals also helps managers stay focused and avoid wasting time on non-essential activities.

Another important strategy is delegation. Managers should delegate tasks to their team members whenever possible. Delegation not only helps managers distribute their workload but also empowers team members to take ownership and develop their skills. By assigning tasks to capable team members, managers can free up their time to focus on more strategic and high-value activities. Effective delegation requires clear communication, trust, and regular follow-up to ensure that tasks are completed on time and to the desired standard.

Time blocking is another effective strategy for managers to manage their time efficiently. Time blocking involves scheduling specific blocks of time for different activities or tasks. By allocating dedicated time slots for specific tasks, managers can minimize distractions and interruptions, allowing them to focus on the task at hand. Time blocking also helps managers create a structured routine and ensures that important tasks are given sufficient attention. It is important for managers to stick to their time blocks and avoid multitasking, as this can lead to decreased productivity and increased stress.

Effective communication is also crucial for effective time management. Managers should communicate clearly and efficiently with their team members, colleagues, and stakeholders. Clear communication helps in setting expectations, avoiding misunderstandings, and minimizing unnecessary back-and-forth. By establishing effective communication channels and providing timely updates, managers can save time and ensure that everyone is on the same page. Regular team meetings, progress reports, and feedback sessions are some effective communication practices that managers can adopt.

Lastly, managers should prioritize self-care and work-life balance. It is important for managers to take breaks, recharge, and maintain a healthy work-life balance. Burnout and fatigue can negatively impact productivity and decision-making abilities. By prioritizing self-care, managers can maintain their energy levels, enhance their focus, and make better use of their time. This can be achieved through activities such as exercise, mindfulness practices, and spending quality time with family and friends.

In conclusion, effective time management is essential for managers to succeed in their roles. By adopting strategies such as setting clear goals and priorities, delegation, time blocking, effective communication, and prioritizing self-care, managers can enhance their productivity, reduce stress, and achieve their objectives. It is important for managers to continuously evaluate and refine their time management strategies to adapt to changing circumstances and maximize their effectiveness.

47- Managing Time for Social Media and Online Activities

Managing Time for Social Media and Online Activities

In today's digital age, social media and online activities have become an integral part of our daily lives. From scrolling through endless feeds to engaging in online discussions, we are constantly connected to the virtual world. However, with the increasing popularity of these platforms, it is crucial to manage our time effectively to ensure a healthy balance between online and offline activities. This essay will explore the importance of managing time for social media and online activities and provide practical tips for achieving this balance.

Firstly, managing time for social media and online activities is essential for maintaining productivity and focus. It is easy to get lost in the vast sea of information and distractions that these platforms offer. Without proper time management, hours can slip away without accomplishing anything meaningful. By setting specific time limits for social media usage and online activities, individuals can allocate their time more efficiently and dedicate their energy to more important tasks, such as work, studies, or personal development.

Secondly, managing time for social media and online activities is crucial for maintaining mental and emotional well-being. While these platforms can provide a sense of connection and entertainment, excessive use can lead to feelings of loneliness, anxiety, and low self-esteem. By establishing boundaries and limiting the time spent on social media, individuals can prioritize real-life interactions, engage in hobbies, and focus on self-care activities. This balance is essential for maintaining a healthy and positive mindset.

Furthermore, managing time for social media and online activities is important for fostering genuine relationships and connections. While these platforms offer the opportunity to connect with a wide range of people, it is crucial to invest time in nurturing meaningful relationships offline. By setting aside dedicated time for face-to-face interactions, individuals can strengthen their bonds with family, friends, and loved ones. These real-life connections provide a sense of belonging and support that cannot be replicated in the virtual world.

To effectively manage time for social media and online activities, it is important to implement practical strategies. Firstly, individuals can establish a schedule and allocate specific time slots for engaging in online activities. By setting clear boundaries, individuals can prevent excessive use and ensure a healthy balance. Secondly, it is beneficial to prioritize tasks and responsibilities before indulging in social media or online activities. By completing important tasks first, individuals can enjoy their online time without the guilt or stress of unfinished work. Additionally, individuals can utilize productivity tools and apps that limit access to social media platforms during specific hours or track time spent online. These tools can serve as reminders and help individuals stay accountable for their time usage.

In conclusion, managing time for social media and online activities is crucial in today's digital world. By effectively managing time, individuals can maintain productivity, focus, and mental well-being. It is important to set boundaries, prioritize real-life interactions, and implement practical strategies to achieve a healthy balance. By doing so, individuals can enjoy the benefits of social media and online activities while still living a fulfilling offline life.

48- Strategies for Effective Time Management for Lawyers

Effective time management is crucial for lawyers to ensure they can handle their workload efficiently and meet their clients' needs. With the demanding nature of legal work, lawyers must employ strategies that allow them to maximize their productivity and minimize stress. In this essay, we will explore various strategies for effective time management for lawyers.

One of the most important strategies for lawyers to manage their time effectively is to prioritize tasks. Lawyers often have multiple cases and deadlines to juggle, so it is essential to identify the most urgent and important tasks and tackle them first. By prioritizing tasks, lawyers can ensure that they allocate their time and resources efficiently and avoid missing crucial deadlines.

Another effective strategy for time management is to create a schedule or a to-do list. Lawyers can benefit from planning their day in advance and allocating specific time slots for different tasks. This helps them stay organized and focused, as they know exactly what needs to be done and when. By following a schedule, lawyers can avoid wasting time on non-essential activities and ensure they are making progress on their cases.

Delegation is another valuable strategy for lawyers to manage their time effectively. Lawyers often have a team of paralegals and support staff who can assist with various tasks. Delegating tasks that do not require their expertise allows lawyers to focus on more critical aspects of their work. By effectively delegating tasks, lawyers can free up their time and increase their overall productivity.

Furthermore, lawyers can benefit from utilizing technology to streamline their work processes and save time. Legal software, document management systems, and communication tools can help lawyers organize and access information efficiently. By leveraging technology, lawyers can automate repetitive tasks, reduce administrative work, and improve collaboration with colleagues and clients.

Effective time management also requires lawyers to set boundaries and manage their workload effectively. It is essential for lawyers to recognize their limitations and avoid taking on more work than they can handle. By setting realistic expectations and communicating their availability to clients, lawyers can prevent burnout and ensure they have enough time to devote to each case.

Lastly, lawyers should prioritize self-care and take breaks to recharge. Working long hours without breaks can lead to decreased productivity and increased stress levels. By incorporating regular breaks, exercise, and leisure activities into their schedule, lawyers can maintain their focus and energy levels, ultimately improving their overall time management.

In conclusion, effective time management is vital for lawyers to succeed in their profession. By prioritizing tasks, creating schedules, delegating, utilizing technology, setting boundaries, and practicing self-care, lawyers can optimize their productivity, reduce stress, and provide quality legal services to their clients. Implementing these strategies will not only benefit lawyers but also contribute to a healthier work-life balance.

49- Managing Time for Personal Reflection and Goal Setting

Managing Time for Personal Reflection and Goal Setting

Time management is a crucial skill that plays a significant role in personal reflection and goal setting. It involves the ability to allocate and prioritize time effectively to achieve desired outcomes. By managing time efficiently, individuals can engage in self-reflection, evaluate their progress, and set meaningful goals for personal growth and development.

One of the key benefits of managing time for personal reflection is the opportunity to pause and evaluate one's actions, thoughts, and emotions. In our fast-paced world, it is easy to get caught up in the daily grind and lose sight of our true desires and aspirations. Taking the time to reflect allows individuals to gain clarity about their values, strengths, weaknesses, and areas for improvement. Through self-reflection, individuals can identify patterns and behaviors that may be hindering their progress and make necessary adjustments.

Furthermore, effective time management enables individuals to set realistic and achievable goals. By allocating dedicated time for goal setting, individuals can identify their short-term and long-term objectives and create a roadmap to achieve them. Setting goals provides a sense of direction and purpose, motivating individuals to work towards their aspirations. When time is managed effectively, individuals can break down their goals into smaller, manageable tasks, making them more attainable and less overwhelming.

In addition, managing time for personal reflection and goal setting helps individuals track their progress and make necessary adjustments along the way. Regularly evaluating one's actions and progress allows individuals to identify areas of improvement and make necessary changes to stay on track towards their goals. By reflecting on past experiences and assessing the effectiveness of their strategies, individuals can refine their approach and increase their chances of success.

Moreover, time management facilitates self-discipline and accountability. When individuals allocate specific time slots for self-reflection and goal setting, they are more likely to follow through and prioritize these activities. By treating these activities as non-negotiable commitments, individuals develop a sense of responsibility towards their personal growth and development. This discipline and accountability contribute to a more focused and productive approach to achieving goals.

In conclusion, managing time for personal reflection and goal setting is essential for personal growth and development. By allocating dedicated time for self-reflection, individuals can gain clarity about their values, strengths, and weaknesses. Effective time management also enables individuals to set realistic and achievable goals, breaking them down into smaller tasks. Regular reflection and evaluation allow individuals to track their progress and make necessary adjustments. Ultimately, by managing time effectively, individuals can cultivate self-discipline and accountability, leading to a more focused and purposeful approach to personal growth and goal achievement.

50- Conclusion: Mastering Time Management for Success

Mastering Time Management for Success

Time is a precious resource that is available to everyone in equal measure. However, not everyone is able to make the most of it. Successful individuals understand the importance of time management and have mastered the art of using their time effectively. In this essay, we will explore the key principles of time management and how it can lead to success in various aspects of life.

One of the fundamental principles of time management is setting clear goals and priorities. Successful individuals know what they want to achieve and prioritize their tasks accordingly. By setting specific, measurable, achievable, relevant, and time-bound (SMART) goals, they are able to focus their time and energy on activities that align with their objectives. This helps them avoid wasting time on unimportant tasks and ensures that they are constantly working towards their desired outcomes.

Another important aspect of time management is planning and organizing. Successful individuals understand the value of planning their days, weeks, and months in advance. They create to-do lists, set deadlines, and allocate time for each task. By having a clear plan in place, they are able to stay organized and avoid procrastination. This allows them to make the most of their time and accomplish more in a shorter period.

In addition to planning, successful individuals also know how to prioritize their tasks. They understand that not all tasks are equally important or urgent. They use techniques such as the Eisenhower Matrix to categorize tasks based on their importance and urgency. This helps them focus on high-priority tasks and delegate or eliminate tasks that are not essential. By prioritizing effectively, they are able to allocate their time and resources in a way that maximizes productivity and ensures that important deadlines are met.

Furthermore, successful individuals are masters of time delegation. They understand that they cannot do everything on their own and that it is important to delegate tasks to others. By delegating tasks to capable individuals, they are able to free up their own time and focus on activities that require their expertise. This not only helps them manage their time more effectively but also fosters collaboration and empowers others to develop their skills.

Another key principle of time management is the ability to minimize distractions. Successful individuals know how to eliminate or minimize distractions that can hinder their productivity. They turn off notifications on their devices, create a conducive work environment, and practice techniques such as time blocking to minimize interruptions. By eliminating distractions, they are able to maintain focus and concentration, leading to higher productivity and better results.

Lastly, successful individuals understand the importance of self-care and work-life balance. They recognize that time management is not just about being productive at work but also about maintaining a healthy and fulfilling personal life. They allocate time for activities such as exercise, relaxation, and spending time with loved ones. By taking care of their physical and mental well-being, they are able to recharge and maintain high levels of energy and motivation, which ultimately contributes to their overall success.

In conclusion, mastering time management is crucial for success in all areas of life. By setting clear goals, planning and organizing, prioritizing tasks, delegating effectively, minimizing distractions, and maintaining a healthy work-life balance, individuals can make the most of their time and achieve their desired outcomes. Time is a finite resource, and those who are able to manage it effectively are more likely to succeed in their endeavors. So, let us all strive to become masters of time management and unlock our full potential for success.

Milton Keynes UK
Ingram Content Group UK Ltd.
UKHW011117100424
440866UK00001B/31